HAUNTED HOMES

Also by Mia Dolan:

The Gift
Mia's World

MIA DOLAN

HAUNTED HOMES

TRUE STORIES OF PARANORMAL INVESTIGATIONS

HARPER
element

HarperElement
An Imprint of HarperCollins*Publishers*
77–85 Fulham Palace Road,
Hammersmith, London W6 8JB

The website address is: www.thorsonselement.com

and *HarperElement* are trademarks of
HarperCollins*Publishers* Ltd

First published by HarperElement 2006

1 3 5 7 9 10 8 6 4 2

© Mia Dolan 2006

Mia Dolan asserts the moral right to be
identified as the author of this work

A catalogue record of this book is
available from the British Library

ISBN-13   978-0-00-722095-3
ISBN-10   0-00-722095-2

Printed and bound in Great Britain by
Clays Ltd, St Ives plc

Contents

Psalm 129: De Profundis

De Profundis clamavi ad te, Domine. Domine, exaudi vocem meam. Fiant aures tuae intendentes, in vocem deprecationis meae. Si iniquitates observaveris, Domine: Domine, quis sustinebit? Quia apud te propitiation est: et propter legem tuam sustinui te, Domine. Sustinuit anima mea in verbo ejus: speravit anima mea in Domino. A custodia matutina usque ad noctem, speret Israel in Domino. Quia apud Dominum misericordia, et copiosa apud eum redemption. Et ipse redemit Israel ex ominibus iniquitatibus ejus.

Out of the depths I have cried to you.
Lord, hear my voice.
Let your ears be attentive to the voice of my petitions.
If you kept a record of sins,
Lord, who could stand?
But there is merciful forgiveness with you,
therefore you are feared.
I wait for the Lord.
My soul waits.
I hope in his word.
My soul longs for the Lord
More than watchmen long for the morning.
Israel, hope in God, for with Him there is loving kindness.
With Him is abundant redemption.
He will redeem Israel from all their sins.

Introduction:

There's More to Life than What We Can See

I used to wish that it would stop. For a long while I thought I was crazy and that other people would think I was crazy too. A hundred years ago I would have been locked up for saying what I believe. That I can tell the future. That I see ghosts. That I have conversations with them and can pass messages to the family and friends they have left behind. Stranger still, I believe that when a ghost is trapped here, in this world, I can help it pass over to the spirit realm. That I have a spirit guide to steer me in all these things. I know it's just weird to most people. It isn't easy being psychic and it isn't always easy for the people around you.

Now I feel lucky. In fact, not only lucky but privileged and honoured. I don't know why this gift has been given to me but I am glad I didn't turn my back on it. I'm glad I took it on.

People think that if you're psychic it comes to you all at once; that you can see everything, know everything, right from the moment your gift is switched on. The truth is that like anything else in life, it takes time to learn what you're seeing and to understand it.

I can talk to spirits directly. That is, I can hear them and engage them in conversation. But I also get visions.

Sometimes the spirit world communicates that way. So instead of telling me that they remember a cellar with stone steps, or that there was a river nearby, sometimes I simply see that. I can smell things too – recently I was in a house and I kept smelling wood smoke and it turned out there had been an open fire some years before, right where I was standing. Other times I feel emotions. I have a sense of things that simply aren't there for other people. I know if a house has been altered in shape or size. I can feel what's happened there. If you give me a family treasure to hold I often sense things from it – love or fights, perhaps. I see the place where that object is normally kept. I can tell how many people have owned it and if it has been passed down from one generation to another.

People often ask me why such specific and strange details come through. Truly, I don't know for sure. Perhaps it is in those fine points that people find comfort. Perhaps it is what helps people believe – a tiny detail that couldn't be guessed, like knowing which finger a certain ring was worn on, or someone's favourite perfume.

First, I became aware of my spirit guide, Eric. I could hear his voice (I thought I was going mad!) and eventually I could see him, though that scared me half to death, of course. I was only twenty-two and I wasn't used to it yet. For a while all I had was snippets of information about people in the street. The certain knowledge that a stranger was pregnant, knowing that someone's left hip was painful or seeing a plane crash but not knowing where it was until I switched on the news. At first that was terrifying, but over time I got used to the randomness of having visions, things coming at me out of nowhere.

And I learnt to control it, like a toddler finding out how to walk in a straight line. It is as if I could grasp my skill and use it to steer myself and see more of what I wanted.

Best, it opens up a new dimension to the world. I can see energy, I suppose you might call it life force energy – auras – the force of light around people. They come in different colours like a light around your body. They tell me about someone's abilities or character. Someone with a lot of green is creative, for example. Someone with a lot of grey is stressed out and probably depressed. It all means that I can help people. I like to help people. In the end that's really the interest for me.

And of course, I can see ghosts. Not only that, I feel them. My heart rate goes up and I can sense the energy. A spirit might be a relation coming with a message for someone they loved. It might be random in that the spirit is only visiting somewhere they knew in life, and have no need for me at all. Other times, like in *Haunted Homes*, there are trapped spirits that haven't passed over and need help to do so. It's a strange feeling but I've never been afraid of it.

Now I spend a lot of time with people who have been bereaved, particularly parents who have lost children. I lost my own son, Shane, when he was eighteen, and I think the gut-wrenching experience of that helps me to relate to other parents going through the same thing. I do believe that when it's your time, it's your time, and you have to go. In the end everyone will have to deal with a death. Everyone is going to lose somebody. And everyone is going to die themselves. That at least is universal. And that's why it's the most important work that I do.

Early in 2004 I was approached by a production company called September Films to do a show for ITV. You'd think I'd have seen it coming but unfortunately, being psychic doesn't work like that. I'm not good at seeing the opportunities coming my way. I can't do it for myself, or at least, my future isn't always clear to me.

I was in London to see my publisher and we ended up going for a drink in a bar in Soho. We were celebrating the first part of my autobiography. It had been in the *Sunday Times* Top Ten and we were chuffed. It was very early on in the springtime but absolutely freezing as I remember it. As we walked down the road I was hugging my coat around me. 'It's in here,' said Katy, my editor, and we went up the steps, in through the door and past the front desk. It was busy in the bar and very flash with lots of muted colours and sofas, and some amazing plants in pots that looked quite exotic. Katy went off and ordered a vodka and tonic for me while I settled down on a sofa, feeling self-conscious. It was exactly the kind of media place I always feel uncomfortable in. I am dead, dead ordinary when it comes down to it. I come from a normal background – we never had much money or anything like that. I often feel I don't fit into the media world. I remember thinking that bar was a bit smart. Everyone was dressed so well, as if their clothes had been chosen specially for them. I am not aware of what I wear. I never know what to fling on and I shifted in my seat, conscious that my scruffy black top and baggy trousers probably weren't winning me any style points. I thought that I would have been much more at ease in a pub somewhere normal, but once Katy and I got chatting I began to relax.

That night I met a producer called Sam Brick, a tall, blonde, beautiful girl from the Midlands. She was wearing a pair of jeans and a big jumper, but still she looked as if she was immaculately turned out. It was eight in the evening and poor Sam was exhausted. I liked her on sight, though, and thought that she would be great to work with.

'Had you thought about doing something on TV?' she asked.

'I would love to but it's difficult to find something that isn't hyped up,' I said.

Sam was interested in producing something with a psychic slant for terrestrial television – something that would be very high quality. We didn't talk for long before she had to go home to bed (I more or less insisted she did – her aura was flat, which only happens when someone is absolutely worn out). But before she went she asked me to do a quick reading for her. I think she was sussing me out – after all, if she was thinking of working with me she had to at least believe in my gift a little.

I settled into the reading, moving from the noisy bar into what I call The Zone, where I am psychically switched on. Basically, I have to tune out the real world and tune into the psychic one. I could see someone who was close to Sam was in the British forces stationed in Iraq and that they had a sore stomach. I saw that she was about to meet someone with whom she would have a great relationship.

'You should jump at that one,' I told her.

I also saw a couple of things about her family, just observations. It all seemed to make sense to her. Often when I give a reading people look slightly bemused but also pleased and excited. I love seeing that look on people's faces. It means whatever I've said has worked for them and feels good. To know someone can really tell what you are about and enter your world is a great sensation. Fortune telling can seem frivolous, I know, but for many people I see it is a real comfort. Sam looked pleased.

'I'm intrigued,' she said. 'That was amazing.' I gave her my number.

A couple of days later Sam rang me at home. She had had time to reflect on her reading and had a few questions so we had a long chat about the kind of work that I do, in particular work with spirits. She was sceptical about that, of course. Most people are.

'You've got something, Mia,' she said. She had been in touch with her friend in Iraq and he had had a stomach problem over the last few days. 'I don't know what it is that you've got, but it's really interesting and I'd like to work with it.'

While Sam was happy to think I might be able to see the future or tell what was going on around her she was slightly uncomfortable with the idea of ghosts. Nonetheless, she decided to pitch three show ideas to ITV around the idea of the supernatural and see what happened. I felt she was a good person so I told her to go ahead.

A couple of weeks later Sam called again. I was sitting in my living room with my feet up and as I picked up the phone I thought I really had to get it together to do some housework. I'm not very interested in housework – just like I am not very interested in fashion.

'One of the ideas I pitched has really taken off,' Sam sounded excited.

'Which one?' I asked. 'What would the show be about?'

The plan was to film me visiting a series of haunted houses. Not stately homes, or places with a particular history. Ghosts don't work like that. In my experience you are as likely to get a haunting in a council house as in a castle – it depends what's happened on the land where the house was built. The film crew would capture me doing my job, essentially. They would find the houses and then I would go and get in touch with the spirits and help them pass over. That was how the idea started.

Over the next couple of weeks I spoke to Sam several more times on the phone.

'It's coming along,' she would always say cheerily.

She put the ideas together and spent a lot of time convincing ITV that the show would work. I enjoyed chatting to her and I found we were good at bouncing ideas off each other. One day Sam phoned from London in a particularly good mood.

'I think we can go to the next stage,' she said. 'You'd better get up here.'

So a few days later I travelled up to meet the production team. It was a lovely day and as I got off the tube at West Kensington and walked to the office the air smelt of hot, fresh bread. There are a couple of really good bakeries on the North End Road and I walked along the busy street enjoying the smell, wondering what was going to happen.

For the meeting, the team had set up a table in the back garden of the office – a small, three-storey, brick terraced house on Vernon Street, near Olympia. They served icy-cold orange juice and we sat in the sun. There were five or six people there as well as me. It was a very relaxed atmosphere. Everyone sat back and lounged. I don't think anyone else around that table believed in ghosts and I wasn't quite sure what to tell them about what I do. You never can be sure what kind of reaction you are going to get. Often people will go so far (believing for example in the 'fortune telling' aspect and open to the idea that their dead grandmother might visit now and again), but then they stop short and are sometimes horrified at the idea of a trapped spirit – someone who can't get across to the spirit world or an entity (that is, a spirit that isn't human). I browsed in my mind while I chatted away, trying to decide just where to pitch this and how to explain it.

Mostly, hauntings are spirits that have been left behind. There are other kinds of ghosts and different beings too. But in the main, if a place is haunted then it's a spirit that has stayed on earth. I believe that when you die a window opens to let you go over to the other side; a portal to take you home to the spirit world. The portal only opens for a limited time and if for some reason you don't use it then you get left behind. It's not easy to cross over once your window has closed. You can't will another opening. So you're stuck. Over time those trapped spirits might inter-act with the human world. Sometimes it is simply their energy that causes what we call 'paranormal phenome-na'. Other times spirits might decide to interact deliber-ately, by moving things, for example. They might be looking for attention or trying to help out. In any event, if you have a spirit around you can get bumps and thumps, temperature changes, plasma, lights, smells or things moving. Those spirits are not evil. In fact, some of them are incredibly good natured.

I once got called out to a haunting near where I live in Kent. The spirit turned out to be an old lady who had been so worried about her husband that she didn't cross over when her time came. She was in the house for years after she died with no sign from her, and then when a young couple moved in she tried to help them by switching out lights when they left a room to save on the electricity. The couple had been in the house a year with that going on, but they had explained it away, deciding the wiring must be faulty. The guy was an electrician and he had checked the wiring over and over and couldn't find anything wrong. Still, they reckoned, there must be some logical explanation, and for the most part they just ignored the irregularities with their lights. Then one evening the old woman had moved a defrosting cake away from the fire because it had been in the warmth long enough. She was trying to help – trying to run the house 'properly'. The young couple had been sitting on the sofa watching TV as the cake floated past them and landed gently, away from the heat. Of course, they were terrified. They had a friend who knew me and made a couple of phone calls to get in touch.

When I arrived at the house they were understandably tense, and more than anything else, seemed embarrassed as they explained to me what had been going on. The guy was sitting back in his chair and whenever he had to speak about what had happened he kept running his hand nervously over his head; stroking his hair for comfort, I suppose. The girl was sitting forward on her chair, her knees together tightly, her lips pursed. She was pretty and had cropped hair. They had bought the place together – for both of them it was their first time buying something and, they explained, they couldn't afford to move out and sell the place on.

The spirit, the old lady, was sweet. I could see that straight away. The atmosphere in the house felt light and pleasant and besides, I could see her behind the sofa, smiling and good natured. She hadn't meant to harm them or scare anyone. She was only trying to help out. She had seen lights on unnecessarily and a cake that was going to spoil in the heat and had done what she probably would have done when she was alive, and fixed things. Those good-natured spirits are often confused. She probably wasn't even aware that she was dead. She had only stayed behind because she was worried her husband wouldn't manage without her.

I watched as a portal opened to the spirit world and the old lady crossed over.

'She was just left behind,' I explained to the young couple, who were, of course, massively relieved that she was gone.

Another time I was contacted by a client whose daughter, son-in-law and baby grandson had been scared witless by the goings on in their house in Sittingbourne. They had actually moved out of the house because there was so much electrical activity, the sound of footsteps going up and down the stairs and constant pacing in one of their bedrooms. When the baby's battery-operated bear started to work all by itself they had had enough. As soon as I arrived at the house I could feel something was there.

The atmosphere was heavy this time – like a pressure in the air. But in the end it was only a man who had been left behind. A good soul. He looked like a typical 1950s, middle-aged bloke – he was wearing a matching waistcoat and trousers and an open-necked shirt with the sleeves rolled up. He told me he was looking for his lady. 'Have you seen her?' he asked me. He must have loved his wife very much. Mostly he just seemed confused and I don't think he had set off the bear deliberately, I expect his energy simply affected the battery. He wasn't aware of the family in the house but was completely engrossed in his search – lost in his own thoughts and emotions.

I've found that if I can simply locate the spirit then my spirit guide can open a portal and they can go over to the spirit world. In both of these cases that's exactly what I did and the spirits went over willingly. As the portal opened I saw a look of recognition on their faces as if to say, 'Ah, that's where I ought to have been.' In a sense I suppose it was what they were really looking for. They were nice people who had stayed only because of their concern and love for their partners. In time that kind of ghost would simply disappear, of course. They would go over naturally – almost dissolve. It's not that they'd be trapped forever. I've never seen or met a trapped spirit more than a couple of hundred years old. It doesn't ring true to me when you hear stories on TV or radio of older spirits interacting with the world – anything much older is a different thing all together. An imprint, maybe. A loop in time. A different kind of mistake, but not a haunting. That kind of ghost is a bit like a photograph and there's nothing you can do to get rid of it, nothing really needing to be done.

But if I can help the spirit of someone who is trapped, then they will go over sooner and it rectifies their mistake in not crossing when they should have. Earth is a place to learn lessons, to have experiences, to try things out and hopefully to grow. The spirit world is home, though, and no-one's soul is meant to be left behind here.

At the meeting in the garden in Vernon Street the production team were both sceptical and keen for drama at the same time. This was a job for them like any other. If you work in a TV company I suppose you don't have to like food to do a cookery programme, or care about the World Cup to organize football coverage. I was just a part of their job to produce good TV. They were delighted I was female because there were so many male TV psychics working at that time. It was about marketing for them. But that was OK. I decided to be quite up front in the end and gave a brief outline of the kind of spirits I had encountered before on hauntings. I have to admit they looked pretty nonplussed. One guy just kept staring at the herbaceous border and looked pretty worried. It didn't bother me in the slightest. I am used to people thinking that I'm weird. After all, I liked what they were proposing. I thought it had a substance. It was real.

The idea for a ghost-busting programme had developed since Sam and I had first spoken. Now they planned to put together a team who would go along with me. There would be a Professor of Paranormal Psychology (who would also be a sceptic) and a technical team of paranormal investigators who would be able to document scientifically what was going on in the houses. All the experts would interview the family who lived there and we would spend two nights in the house, looking for evidence of the haunting. Then I would send the spirit over to the other side and the family could continue with their lives again. It was set to be the first programme of its kind on terrestrial TV, though similar things had been done before on cable. We called it *Haunted Homes*.

The more I thought about it the more I liked it. I liked that the situation wasn't unusual for me and that it wasn't contrived in any way. I often get called out to hauntings so it is familiar territory. In the normal run of things I get around ten calls a week from people who think they have a ghost in their home, although most of them turn out to have overactive imaginations for one reason or another. People can scare themselves silly sometimes and there isn't anything supernatural involved. I learned very early on that a scared person on the phone doesn't necessarily mean a paranormal problem. Nine times out of ten it is either something completely rational or else something in the mind of the caller. I might deal with ten or fifteen genuine cases a year. This would simply add a few more to my roll call.

On my way home on the train, I realized that it was perfect – the idea seemed to work for everyone involved. It was a good thing to do for the spirits because they were trapped and shouldn't be there. It was good for the families who were scared out of their wits. The TV crew would get what they wanted. And for me, well, I liked the idea of a technical team. People who could measure and clarify what I can only feel would be fantastic. What a great way to communicate with an audience – to open up their minds to the idea that something is out there – to have me sense something and then look for scientific proof of it. Perfect. The thing is, I don't just *believe* in a spirit world, I *know* it is there. A belief is something that can be shaken. For me the spirit world is an absolute certainty. And that knowledge has changed my life. I can't imagine losing a child and not being sure that there was more to it. Of seeing your brother, sister, mother or father die and thinking that was the end. It would make death even more devastating.

Perhaps more important than that, if you believe in an afterlife, that you will be called to account for the kind of life you lead, then you have to take a serious look at how you're living. I like nice things as much as the next person, but the material world is less important than the emotional and spiritual worlds. If I can make people think about that; wonder if there is more to life than superficial needs and wants, that's important to me. It could be a wake up call for someone who needs one. I've done readings for gangsters and criminals, for paedophiles and wife-beaters. If you're truly convinced there is more to life, if you're truly convinced you'll be called to account, then you have to re-evaluate the way you live. It can bring about the most astonishing changes in people. I've seen it happen.

One time a heroin addict came to see me. He wanted to kill himself and had come to me to check what might happen. It sounds strange, I know, but he was at the end of his tether, tortured and miserable and desperate. He could see the havoc he was inflicting on the people around him, the hurt he had caused not only to himself but to his family and friends. He couldn't bear it any more. I truly believe that no one is given a problem that they don't somewhere have the resources to manage. The idea of life is to be stretched to the limit. Everyone's limit is different. He must have been very strong to have been sent this kind of test. I talked to this man for hours – I think we stayed up half the night.

'Don't give up,' I kept saying. 'If you give up you won't have learned the lesson you need to learn. You will have to start learning it a second time. It will happen all over again to you. You've come so far and you need to get through this. You need to move on with your life and because of what you have been through, instead of hurting the people around you, maybe you can help them.'

This man didn't kill himself. He gave up drugs and through his own bravery turned his life around. He became a social worker and specialized in drug dependency problems. I remember feeling proud of him, tremendously proud, that he'd come so far. That he could really help others because of his own experiences. He is someone who has made a difference with his life.

That's what I mean. Once you know that there is an afterlife, that you will be called to account, that your troubles and difficulties are the measure of the way you live and the kind of person you are, it brings amazing changes. That man had given up hope and in the end he believed in himself enough to turn himself around. I wanted to do the TV series because even if it could only reach one person, and help one person (though of course, I'd hope for more), that one person would make a huge difference. So the best thing I could hope for was proof. Something to sway the cynical and, in the end, bring people hope. If there is an afterlife then you have to change the way you live.

A couple of weeks later I was back in London and I gave the production team a questionnaire I use to classify hauntings, to sort out drink-fuelled imaginings from the real McCoy. They were going to advertise for families willing to invite us in, people who were looking for assistance, and these questionnaires would be a big help to them.

From experience I knew that most families in that situation would be at the end of their tether. I am usually the last port of call – after the police, the electricity board and the local priest. For the TV show we agreed that the spirits would have to have been active over a period of time – a few weeks at least, perhaps even years. Usually hauntings start small, with things that can be explained away or ignored, and then gradually build up into something more tangible. Clearly the production team wanted something as tangible as possible so the supernatural phenomena had to have been experienced by more than one person. It was important that there shouldn't be a history of drink, drugs, psychosis or even heavy medication in the family. Most importantly, I wasn't going to be told anything at all, until I turned up on the day. There had to be no inkling in my mind of what I was going to find, and no way that I could do any advance research. I was going in blind.

'You understand?' Sam said. 'You won't know anything about where you're going, Mia. We'll drop you at the door and you just have to go in there on your instincts alone. We'll know what the families are saying is happening, but you'll have to diagnose it for yourself.'

'Fine,' I said. 'That's great. It gives me a chance to prove myself.'

They decided to shoot a pilot that summer. Then if ITV went ahead and commissioned the series the production would be set up for the following year.

I know I make what I do sound easy. A ghost here and a ghost there. A portal to the spirit world and off we go. I've been psychic for over twenty years and I have spent a lot of time developing my ability to slip into the psychic state. To tune in, I suppose. That means being incredibly relaxed and slipping into a state of being where I subdue my own emotions and simply listen and observe. It isn't totally in my control. I often see spirits whether I want to or not. Sometimes, having sensed that they can communicate with me, a ghost will become insistent. I might be busy and rather not have a chat, but one will arrive that really wants to grab my attention. I have been pushed, shoved and shouted at! Sometimes I can talk to them and hear what they have to say. Sometimes they don't need to speak; I can simply tell what they are about, like I can with people who are alive. I will see images or just get a strong feeling from them. They might be fizzing angry or frustrated and that's how I start to feel. I empathize. I can't truly say that sending spirits to the other side is easy. I only act as an anchor in that respect. I don't make it happen, I am just part of the equation. I locate the spirit and then my spirit guide can come and do the rest. It isn't easy, though. I cry almost every time. It is an amazing experience with very heightened emotions. It is intense and it does affect me. Afterwards, I feel a mixture of elation and exhaustion.

I would never want to leave someone trapped; I always want to help them over to where they belong. The spirit world is something essentially natural and part of being human, I believe, and I am never afraid when I am in contact with spirits. But I have also experienced things which are unnatural and evil; things which are not human, not of the spirit world. Dark forces do exist and in dealing with them I do get scared. That's an understatement. I get petrified. Close to paralyzed. Scared stiff. And then I have to fight that feeling because in the end, evil entities feed on fear. It only makes them stronger.

You have to understand, I'm not talking about a human spirit that's grumpy, angry or simply mischievous. Some of those get trapped, of course. They don't want to go over because they sense they may be made to face what they've done, the kind of people they've been. That's common but not scary. I'm not talking about poltergeist activity either. That's psychic energy out of control – a teenager who has some natural abilities but does not yet have the measure of them, or sometimes one of those angry, trapped spirits playing up out of badness.

I'm talking about Evil with a capital. And that scares me. I have seen it and felt it. My heart rate rising, my heart pounding, a feeling of coldness and pure dread. It is all consuming and you want to bolt, to get away at any cost. When you are in the presence of Evil there is a sense of power, a sense of the absolute and a sense of badness; malevolence that is so all encompassing that your blood seems to go cold and a heavy weight lies on your heart. There is Evil beyond anything human. I know it exists. I don't know about the Devil or his minions, I don't know about Hell and brimstone and fury, I just know what I've experienced, the encounters I'm about to explain.

In the end I always trust my feelings. I know there are places outside the physical world, different realms, if you like. There is the spirit world itself – the place where we go in spirit after we die. Then there is another realm – a place of pure evil, completely separate from the spirit realm. It isn't human. I've seen the portal open to the good place. I know there is a bad place too. I also believe in the existence of absolute goodness – not in a God with a big, white beard – but in a force of goodness that is complete, also beyond anything human. The good news is that it is very, very rare for something truly Evil to exist on earth and when that happens it isn't what I'd call a ghost. It goes well beyond anything a ghost could do.

I only consciously made contact with that once. I was very young and had only just started out on my psychic career. I think I was arrogant more than anything and I had been asked to see what I could do for a psychic investigator in Kent, where I live. I remember turning up to a flat in Sheerness – somewhere completely normal. It was someone's home. I had done some readings the week before and the psychic investigator had been pleased. Now she wanted to see if I could 'manifest' something. She wanted me to call up a spirit. I was eager to show her what I could do. This was the first time I had met someone who had been published – this woman was writing a book and if I succeeded I was going to be in it. I desperately wanted to shine. Sometimes I can be a bit of a show off, I know.

My spirit guide, Eric, had warned me against trying to manifest a spirit, but I wanted to be able to prove something was out there, and after all, at the time, I had only ever experienced human spirits. I had no idea. It was dark – a winter evening – and there were nine of us in the room. I had brought along a friend.

I remember everyone forming a circle and then I remember pulling in a couple of deep breaths and getting to work. The memory is so vivid it's as if I am there ...

The group is expectant and nervous in a light-hearted, giggly way. No one is afraid. Rather than just waiting, as I normally do, to see what I can observe, I focus my energy and I call out mentally into The Zone – the place I go to sense the paranormal, the place where I can see things beyond the physical world. I am inviting something to come. And it does.

First, the light on the side table goes out and the room falls into darkness except for a street lamp outside the window. The circle is shaken, everyone is looking around. Immediately I know that I have made a mistake. I flash panic.

'Oh no,' I whisper. 'This feels wrong.'

Something is coming and it isn't a normal spirit. It isn't human. I know it's a cliché but I can see a black dog at the top of a set of stairs. An old man's face is transposed onto one of the women's faces on the other side of the circle. The atmosphere feels awful. Everyone in the room can feel it too. I know this being is different from a human ghost – there is a heavy, dark dread in the pit of my stomach, I have icy hands and an ominous sensation that things are about to go very wrong. Tingling.

A voice, a male voice, from outside the room, says, 'It's coming.'

My forehead is clammy, a creeping sensation. I hear the male voice say, 'You do not know what you have done.' And then it is here. It is in the room.

This entity wants to feed on fear. It is emerging out of a shadowy place, ominous and threatening. It wants to escape from where it has been. It wants to be in the world. To it, the world means freedom to exercise its nature. I can see it. Looming. A dark shape, almost human. It looks heavy, awkward and ominous. This thing is after us, black and on the prowl, circling around malevolently behind our backs. It feels terrifying. My heart is pounding. I have goosebumps, creeping flesh. Everyone in the circle is disturbed as they look around frantically with foreboding. Someone next to me is panting with terror. We can all feel it. The soul of destruction. Terror. Then one of the women in the circle loses her nerve completely and tries to make a break for it but I know that she has to stay. Whatever happens, everyone has to stay.

'Don't split the circle,' I shout and she is pulled back into place.

Nauseous with panic, I don't think I can hold this for long. I have called this dark being and it is up to me to send it back. Right now. It has to go now. I have to take control and stand up to it. If it stays it will only get stronger and visit untold harm. This creature wants to hurt and destroy. It is a black and dreadful thing with no humanity in it, it is sizing us up, it is prowling around us, very close now. It is a heavy, black shape and we are its prey. It wants fear. It wants harm. I am sick to my stomach. I have to fight my terror more than anything and stand firm.

Occasionally it happens that human spirits don't want to leave. Then you have to hold on tight, keep them there and let the spirit guides do what's best for them. This is a different situation completely. Whatever is in the room is Evil and it doesn't want to leave even though it doesn't belong here. It has a dark, dark purpose.

With my heart pounding so hard that it is painful and my hands weak with terror I am relieved to see my spirit guide arrive. I am not sure I can manage this. I am not sure how much he can help me; if what I can do will be enough. This being is strong and it doesn't want to leave. At once my spirit guide says gently, 'Concentrate on the cross.' For a few seconds I panic. I can't see a cross, then in the darkness it appears glowing dimly with a pale, yellow light. I focus on it and the light becomes stronger and whiter. The feeling of dread fluctuates, getting stronger and weaker as the creature, whatever it is, moves around the room with malice as if it is on the hunt. It's behind me. Right behind me. The temperature has plummeted and everyone in the circle is petrified. I can see their faces, all tense, all terrified. I focus on the cross, I fight to retain the image of it before my eyes. This creature wants to stay, and by standing up to it I am telling it to leave. I am going to make it leave. There is no place for it here. No place on earth. I am plagued, doubting my ability, struggling with whether it is worth it or not. I feel exhausted and I want to give up. Fingers of fear lay themselves on me, running chills up my spine, but I hold firm. I don't give up. I am not going to give up. I am determined that it is going to leave. I am straining. Holding on. And then, at last, there is a sudden flash of light and the Evil is gone.

The lamp splutters and comes back on. Everyone in the room looks pale and tense. One woman, so weakened by the experience, holds onto a chair and then sinks down into its pillows. No one says anything at first. Everyone just wants to get out of that flat. Eventually the woman who lives there says, 'I can't stay here any more. I have to move house.' And then the psychic investigator comes up to me. She is grinning.

'That was amazing,' she says. 'Shall we say same time next week?'

Some people don't understand how serious it is. Some people don't understand that it isn't a game. Going into a house that's haunted I know I might meet that dark being again. You have to be prepared every time.

Happily it is rare. I have often turned up at someone's house and they think the presence they feel is evil. That is only their fear talking. It's easy to become terrified of something you don't understand. Some spirits might be unpleasant. You can get a heavy feeling, a depressed feeling, from someone who is frustrated and trapped. They simply might not have been a nice person and that stays with them in death.

Mostly, though, they are confused. A trapped spirit will appear as they were when they died. Often they are in their pyjamas. That's different from a ghost who is visiting, someone who has passed over and is going through the process of coming to terms with their lives. Those spirits appear as if they were in their prime. They are only visiting fleetingly, and they won't haunt you, not like a trapped spirit might. A trapped spirit may be bored and frustrated and looking for attention or out for trouble.

In contrast, from visiting spirits I usually get a sense of peace. I saw my Nan once, in my house. I was doing a reading for someone else and I thought she had come to visit them, rather than me. I described her but the client didn't recognize the description and I didn't recognize her myself. My Nan had lived to be in her eighties but this spirit was no more than thirty. She was wearing a beautiful 1940s blue formal dress with a belt around the pinched-in waist. I think the dress was silk.

'Odd,' I thought. 'I wonder who that is,' and as it seemed to have no bearing on the reading I was doing, I moved on to the other things I could see, the client's relationship, her sons and the fact she was moving house.

The ghost smiled and twirled round. I kept focusing on the reading and the image disappeared.

I didn't know who the spirit had been until I told my mother what I'd seen. She recognized her own mother, of course. The dress had been one of my grandmother's favourites; the swirly blue pattern was very distinctive. She had brought that dress, among others, with her from Italy when she had married my grandfather after the war. I wish now that I had stopped the reading and that I had acknowledged her, maybe spoken to her. I was focused on the other person, you see. But I would have liked to have seen if she had anything to say to me, any message to pass on. She looked happy, at least. Her spirit was young, and very, very beautiful. It must have been the prime of her life.

My brother died a few years ago. It was totally unexpected, a horrible shock. I had seen that he was going to be involved in something violent on a night out in town and I'd tried to warn him. I hadn't known he would be hurt so very badly. And besides, if it is your time, then it's your time. There's nothing anyone can do. I was worried though. I was on edge. It's terrible when you know something is going to happen to someone you love and there isn't any action you can take to prevent it.

His girlfriend had just had a baby and they were out in Sheerness one evening, in a pub. He was trying to help a young guy he knew who had got into a fight over a spilt drink. Pete was a big bloke, you would have thought he was pretty invincible. He was a kind person, although he could be a bit of a rogue. When the fight started he tried to stop it, but he couldn't and in the end he was stabbed. Even with a bad wound he had to make sure everyone was all right; that was Pete. He staggered around injured making sure his girlfriend was OK. Later, the doctors couldn't figure out how he had managed that because it was a very bad injury and he should really have died much more quickly. But Pete was always like that – he had to be sure that everyone was safe. He didn't die until he got to the hospital and the news came to me a short time afterwards, when I was at home. I remember wanting to protect my mother from the pain. I remember feeling numb and disbelieving and angry all at once. My other brother, Jed, and I had to identify Pete's body. We didn't want to leave that to Mum. I don't think she could have borne it.

In life Pete and I were close and I have seen him several times since he died. I have recurring dreams about him. I am walking up a hill in the sunshine and Pete is waiting for me at a gate. Everything is green and beautiful. Strangely, though, we are up high, but there isn't a view. There isn't anything except the hill. I feel excited to see him. It's so nice to see him again. We walk further up the slope for a while and sit in an outdoor café with white tables and chairs. Pete gives me advice about what is going on and tells me what's for the best. It might be family problems, advice about my daughter, or something to do with his daughter, Francesca, who lives with me. Sometimes we just laugh like we used to when we were kids. Then we walk back to the gate and he hugs me goodbye. I can feel him. I can feel a real body. He is the same age he was when he died and in good shape – very strong and comforting. Then I go back down the hill again. Perhaps that's only a dream, though. I have it a lot – maybe once or twice a year. It seems real enough to me.

Pete visits me in my waking life too, but not when he first died. Most spirits can't come back to earth for the first couple of years after they pass over. They aren't ready. Pete helped me when I did my first big, live show. I looked out from the stage and spotted him in the hall, standing there grinning at me. Then he dotted around the audience and chose people for me to give readings to.

'This one, sis,' he said. 'And then that old lady over there.'

Just knowing he is there, on my side, makes a huge difference to me.

On several occasions he's given me advice – good advice. I believe he's brought me good luck too. He visited me in hospital once when I was ill and made me realize how precious life is and how I had to hold on to mine. That life force energy is beautiful and magical. It's a gift we're all given, a miraculous spark, and mostly people forget about it and don't realize that we're lucky just to be alive. Every day we're here we ought to be aware of how special our time is. I miss my brother a lot. He died young and there are so many things that I would like to have shared with him. Day to day things he would have been there for – birthdays and Christmas, Sunday lunches and long phone calls in the evenings – normal stuff. But despite those emotions I'd never call his spirit. For reasons that will become clear later in this book, you can't do that. You just don't know what you'll get if you invite a spirit. It isn't possible to be specific and only invite the ghost you want. If you send out an invitation you don't have control over it and you don't know what you will get back.

I do understand why someone who had been bereaved would want to do that though. I can identify with the impulse. I've lost people who have been close to me and I have been desperate too. I understand when people come to see me and they're frantic for an explanation or even just for some news from someone who has died. I've had people travel thousands of miles for that. For a reason why it happened, perhaps, or to know that the person they loved is all right.

When you are faced with that kind of pain it's easy to dismiss other people who come for something more trivial. A lot of clients turn up to find out about their love lives or to see if they might get a promotion at work. But I try to remember that what's serious for one person is less so for another. Someone who has been dumped or lied to by someone they love is still in pain. Someone who's lonely is hurting too and perhaps they have a lesson to learn which I can help with. Everyone is on a different journey and all those journeys are important. Every single person who comes to me is part of my journey, too, whether that experience is pleasant or unpleasant. Life doesn't fling anything at us that somewhere inside we don't have the resources to handle and I have seen people take on amazing challenges and come out the stronger for it. We should all try to help each other if we can.

The most difficult thing I have had to face was a demonic haunting. Until *Haunted Homes* it was my only other experience of Evil. I know when I tell these stories I make it sound as if Sheerness and Kent are the paranormal capitals of the world. As I have become better known I have been asked to places outside my home county, sometimes even abroad. For the TV series we filmed all over the UK. But the majority of my experience is close to home. When you are psychic, most things come to you by word of mouth so it's only to be expected. For the record, Kent is in my opinion no more or less haunted than anywhere else.

I had never experienced anything as powerful as this haunting – this demonic entity. At base my life is normal. I spend time with my mother. We live together – my mother, myself, my daughter Tanya and my niece Francesca. I am happy. I suppose most people are like that – involved with their family and close friends, just living in their homes and mostly enjoying their lives. Going to the gym. Watching TV. Working. Cooking some food. Being psychic I have an extra dimension. It's like walking around with the radio on, but most of the time not really listening to it. I have five and a half senses unless I choose to really switch on the sixth. But that is normal for me. I am just normal.

I got a call from my friend Belinda. She knew someone who thought they had a poltergeist. The guy, David, was terrified, she said. He had a business in Iwade, about ten miles from my home. Would I go over straight away? Usually I do qualify people first – have a chat over the phone and make sure they aren't on heavy medication or completely drunk out of their heads – but for some reason, in this case I just drove straight over there.

I remember it being a gorgeous summer day and I was listening to the radio as I motored along with the windows down. The address was a warehouse away from the main road. It looked like a scrappy old barn with scrubland all around it. David's business is in wholesale food and he supplies distribution for pet shops. His van was parked outside the warehouse. I pulled up next to it and switched off my engine. A tall, rangy guy came walking out of the main door followed by an Alsatian and a long-haired, black Labrador. He looked worried as he waved to greet me. I got out of the car.

'Are you David?' I asked.

He shook my hand. 'Yes,' he said. 'Thanks for coming over. It's been mad in this place. We could really use your help.'

We sat down outside on some old chairs that were lying out in the sun. David told me what had been going on. His dogs used to sleep in his office and it all started when he was in there working. Both the animals suddenly jumped up and started barking and growling at the corner of the room. Then they stopped for a minute and instead of barking, they whimpered in fear and cowered down for a few moments before they ran out of the office and refused to come back in.

'I wondered what on earth had got into them,' David said, his face bright with the sunlight, 'but I wasn't worried. I didn't think about it too much, to be honest. I was busy.'

Then, a few days, later the electrics started playing up. Lights went off and on again, the electric till flew open for no reason and then slammed shut. The radio David usually had playing would change stations on its own. That went on for a while. After a bit, the local stray cats, that David had fed every day since he had taken over the place, stopped coming in for their food.

Then one day David went into the storage area at the back of the warehouse and some very large, very heavy containers had been moved right across the room. 'Normally you would have needed machinery to do that,' he said. 'I didn't see how anyone could have shifted them without me knowing. And there was no reason to, anyway.'

Carrie, David's assistant, was only eighteen. Like him, she had been looking for a rational explanation for all these problems. Both of them had spent weeks being dismissive and ignoring what was going on. Then one day Carrie saw the outline of a black figure. It was a rough silhouette of a person coming out of the office area and moving across the floor. Then it disappeared completely, right in front of her. She was beside herself with fear but David was convinced it was only her imagination until a few days later when he saw the same figure himself. He was sitting at the desk, working on his computer and out of the corner of his eye he saw the dark, rough-edged shape of a man come through the door towards him. It stood there for a second and then it was gone. As soon as he'd seen it for himself he realized he should have taken Carrie's worries seriously.

'I had the worst feeling, then,' he said. 'Mia, it was awful. So heavy and black. It's difficult to describe.'

I am perfectly accustomed to people being scared, but this sounded different from that. Something wasn't quite normal about this haunting. I asked David more about the feeling he'd had.

'It's hard to explain,' he carried on, 'like it was the heaviest sense of fear I have ever felt. It came out of nowhere and it was a hundred times more frightening than any of the strange things that had happened. It wasn't only weird, or annoying, or a bit freaky. Like the lights going on and off again. It was just very, very bad. It was like Dread. Do you know what I mean?'

I nodded. What David was saying sounded very much like what I had felt in the flat in Sheerness all that time ago. Mind you, you never know. It could have been anything.

'Well, I'd better take a look,' I said, and I smiled to put him at his ease. 'Let's go inside.'

Inside, the warehouse was very tidy, clean and well organized. There were stacks of cans, packets and boxes on rows of shelves that were lit by overhead bulbs. It had a nice feel to it – the sensation of a place that is orderly and well looked after. As we came in I couldn't sense anything supernatural or scary at all. Then, as I got nearer to the office area, past all the shelves, I became uneasy. When I put out my hand to open the office door it hit me like a wall of static electricity all at once. It felt like vibrating, gut-wrenching dread and it shook through my whole body. I instinctively stepped back from the doorway. This wasn't just a mischievous spirit. It was too malevolent for that. This was Evil. I could feel it.

I turned to David. 'The problem's coming from inside your office,' I said.

'Can you get rid of it?'

I nodded. 'I'll try. It's not a normal ghost but I have done something like this before. It was a long time ago.'

I could already feel, though, that this was stronger than what had materialized in the flat in Sheerness those years ago when the lights had gone out and the feeling of malevolence had pervaded the room. This was something that had taken root. It had been there for a while and had been able to feed off the atmosphere of ill-ease and terror it had created. Each time it fed it got stronger.

I knew what I needed to do and I steeled myself. The main thing is not to get frightened. A bad entity will cause as much fear as possible and then it will feed off that emotion. The spirit world is all about emotions. Emotion is the energy the spirit world runs on. The good feeling that you get between friends – that's creative energy. That's energy that can nurture you. This energy felt deadly; it was a deathly force. It needed negative emotions to grow. It wanted only bad things. It was destructive and hard. And it wasn't human. Nothing good could come of it. I knew it shouldn't be there.

I called Eric, my spirit guide. He appeared as usual, a scruffy looking monk in his eighties.

'You need to anchor it,' he said. 'You need to tune into it and pull it towards you. If you can hold it there, I can help.'

It looked like this time the cross wasn't going to appear. Perhaps sometimes the cross isn't enough or maybe at the time when I had seen the cross it had been put there as a symbol for me. Something familiar for me to hold on to. It was many years later now and through my experiences I had left a lot of my Catholic upbringing behind. I shifted my feet, cleared my mind and centred myself. I would have to summon all my inner strength and tap into my absolute belief in the power of good to be able to take this on.

My skin was raised in goosebumps. The hairs were standing up on my arms. I could still feel the sense of evil and foreboding emanating from the door of the office. My heart was racing. I took a couple of deep breaths, opened the door and walked into the room. It was like walking into a storm. I could feel the energy of the entity buffeting me. A chilly, icy fear crept up on me and I had to fight it off. Then a dark shape appeared. It was about the size of a man, maybe six feet tall. It oozed ill will, and it moved slowly towards me. It felt as if it was getting bigger.

'Perhaps I'm not strong enough. Perhaps I won't be able to keep control,' I thought.

David was right, I realized. It is very difficult to describe what it feels like to be in the presence of something like that. It is like being weakened, having something trying to hook in to you with no regard for your wishes or feelings. It feels as if you are being used and manipulated and you have no choice even though you know it is bad. It is like having something taken from you. And you're terrified, or at least, terror is your instinctive response. I was shaking as a feeling of hate filled my heart. It was horrible and it felt a lot like panic. It was making me feel like this to weaken me – to get its hooks into me. I couldn't trust what I was feeling – dread, distilled. I knew I couldn't let it take hold. The moment I allowed fear to really paralyze me would be the moment it could get inside. I had to enforce my will, to turn my thoughts around and focus on my belief in goodness to give me strength. I was rocking in and out of control, battling the energy down. I could feel my body sweating and shaking and I just kept pushing for what I wanted. I was determined. This thing shouldn't be here, I said to myself. This thing can only cause harm. Then suddenly I felt the power shift and I had it. Somehow it was under control. I was holding it.

'Keep strong. Don't waver,' I heard Eric say. He was right beside it now.

I couldn't even reply. Doing this was taking every scrap of energy that I had. It was too important to keep my attention absolutely focused. I couldn't move, couldn't speak and couldn't think about anything else.

Then I noticed something odd. Or at least something I had never seen before. Eric was with another spirit guide. In all the years I had never seen that. Eric is very old but this man was younger. He was wearing robes like Eric's too – though this spirit guide didn't have his head shaved or carry a rosary. He and Eric were either side of the entity. I was waiting for a portal to open, like when you send a spirit across. I knew, though, that this portal would have to be to a different place. This would be a window into somewhere dark. But the spirit guides hesitated a moment and nothing opened at all. Instead, both Eric and his companion turned towards the blackness and raised up huge rods of light that went up to the ceiling. They started to move inwards, towards each other. They were moving very slowly and as they did so the black shape contorted and became even darker as if it was trying to push out against the engulfing light. It was a struggle with the dark shape pushing against them but they kept moving closer to each other, tiny step by tiny step, until at last the rods came together, there was a flash of light and the thing was gone.

I backed towards the door and went back outside to David. A breeze was billowing through the wide warehouse doors and I sank down gratefully onto a wooden chair. My face was dripping with sweat and I was shaking from the exertion. I could feel tears around my eyes. I think I had been crying. I felt as if I had sidestepped something awful, as if that thing would have violated me and hurt me badly. Most of all, I wanted a cigarette but I was shaking so much I didn't think I would be able to hold one. I'd certainly never have been able to light one anyway.

'Was that a poltergeist?' David asked.

I wondered what he heard from outside the office. If he had seen the bright light when the rods came together.

'A poltergeist?' I replied. 'No, it bloody wasn't.'

Once I had recovered enough we went to the pub up the road to steady my nerves further. David, it turned out, hadn't seen anything from the other side of the office door. It is a plywood door with a small square of safety glass. He hadn't looked through, though. He had only heard me huffing and puffing – the sound of someone having a fit inside the room – but he hadn't seen the light underneath the door or through the glass. I was not surprised. Mostly people don't see the things that I do. I'm used to it. On the other hand, he said that he felt a creeping, gripping, physical sensation of fear while he was outside waiting. His hands were icy and his heart was pounding the whole time I was in there. It only stopped when I came out. Now he seemed a bit dazed.

'Has it gone?' David pressed me. 'Are you absolutely sure?'

'Yes. It's gone. I know that as a certainty.'

'And can it come back?' he pushes. 'What if it comes back?'

'It's gone. That's it. But if you have any other problems then call me. Put your mind at rest though – it isn't there any more. Really.'

That isn't what actually concerned me, though. At this point I was focusing on something else. I was worried about how that thing got into the warehouse in the first place. Evil doesn't roam the Earth unbidden. It just doesn't work like that.

'David,' I said, 'I need to know how that thing got there.'

He shrugged his shoulders. 'I have no idea,' he says.

'Could anyone have been using the warehouse once you

had closed for the night? Could anyone have done a ouija board sitting – anything like that? A séance or something?'

'No. The place is alarmed and no-one could get in there without setting it off. I've never done anything like that – and same goes for Carrie, I'm sure of it. But before I took the place over it did lie empty for a while and I heard that there was a crowd of teenagers who used to hang out there at night and mess about. It was a while ago. The guy who rented it to me said they had scared themselves silly somehow and that they wouldn't be back. I didn't think anything of it. But that was a couple of years ago now. That thing couldn't have been there all that time, could it? Just hanging around?'

It probably was a ouija board, I reckoned. I decided that those kids were lucky to get away. They probably didn't come face to face with it. I don't think that happened. They just had a bad feeling or two and fled as it prowled the room, like the entity in the flat in Sheerness had done. When you're faced with that kind of thing your instinctive reaction is to get away – just to run. After that, it had stayed in the warehouse, lying dormant for a while until David's dogs had sensed it. It had been biding its time. Maybe building strength slowly.

It is certainly the worst thing I have ever had to deal with, and definitely the worst thing I have ever felt.

I've heard stories – only one or two – about what can happen if you aren't prepared and you call something like that to you. I've heard what happens if you can't battle off an entity like that. I believe that people have died, the police desperately searching for a rational explanation for their murder. I heard of one case thirty years ago in Aberystwyth. This was before I was psychic and I was staying nearby for the summer – I was just a kid. A friend of the family I was staying with knew the people involved. They were two students, young guys, who had thought they could control whatever they called up. They had been studying Satanism as part of a college project in history and it had fascinated them. Their story reminds me of that psychic investigator in Sheerness who didn't realize that it wasn't a good idea to call up an entity every week so she could write her book – people who don't realize that it isn't just 'interesting'. There are things out there that are Evil. Those beings can cause real harm.

The boys in Aberystwyth had locked themselves into a room in their house and sent their girlfriends out to the pub for the evening. They wanted to be alone to experiment. They said they were going to call up the Devil himself. When the girls came home after closing time, the room was silent, still locked, and they went upstairs to bed, thinking nothing of it. The next morning the door was still locked and the girls decided to break in. What they saw inside was horrifying. The room was covered in blood. Those poor kids' bodies had been minced till there was nothing recognizable left. And they were in a room that had been sealed. There was no logical explanation for it. I remember the police saying that some lunatic must have got in there, but the door was locked from the inside and the windows blocked up so that doesn't make sense. No one was ever caught or charged for those murders. That summer we heard that the girls who had found what was left of the bodies had to undergo a lot of counselling and one of them was admitted to hospital for a while. No one could understand what had happened. Personally, given the circumstances, I don't think whatever did that was human.

I remember a girl who visited me once. She was a very pretty black girl who said her brother had been involved with black magic. He had been heavily involved in ritual magic and obsessed with Satanism. A few months before she came to see me the poor guy had died of an unexplained heart attack. He had only been in his twenties and had seemed completely fit and healthy. She told me that he had spent the days before his death babbling that 'something is coming'. He had been obsessed by the occult and calling up the Devil and had been performing ceremonies with his friends. After he died she was terrified that whatever she believed had killed him would come after her.

'I feel that it's going to be me next,' she said tearfully.

This girl had left her home town. She was having difficulty sleeping and was hysterical. After some time I calmed her down. She hadn't been involved in any way and I knew she would be safe. She just had to stay away.

So, whether you believe in good and evil or not, here are a couple of pieces of advice. First, when you die, there will be a light. That is your portal, that is your opening to get into the spirit world and it won't stay open for a long time. Go into it and someone you know and love will come to meet you. When you die, go over into the light. Don't stay behind.

Secondly, don't play with the spirit world. In particular, don't try out a ouija board. Evil can't come into your life unless it's invited. Neither can good for that matter, though I've never heard of anyone calling up an angel

with a ouija board. I'm not saying that every time someone sets up a board they will call up Evil; it's just that you
don't know what you will get when you open that portal.
It's not a game and it's not worth the risk.

If you want to experiment, then try speaking to your
spirit guide, because you definitely have one. Try seeing
auras around people in the street. Let your mind go limp
and see what you feel when you look at someone: check
out their bodies for illness; visualize them with someone
to see if they're in a relationship. All of that is harmless.
But whatever you do, don't try to contact the dead, even if
it's someone dear, someone you've loved. That's not within your gift or mine. A ghost may choose to visit you –
someone you've loved and known may come back to see
you. Most times you won't see them. It's part of them coming to terms with their lives, and if you do see them it
might be that they have some advice for you, some sage
words for a difficult time. That's not impossible. But you
shouldn't try to contact them, if for no other reason than
you don't know what you might call up.

There are dark, dark forces. I believe those entities,
those beings, can only cause harm – it is their sole purpose. You need to treat the occult with a lot of respect.
So no ouija boards, no black magic ceremonies. It's too
risky. You don't know what you'll get. Please, please just
stay away from it.

People often ask me about my spirit guide, Eric. I am not
keen on the term 'guardian angel' but I suppose that's
what he is. For years I didn't tell anyone that I had a
spirit guide. It seemed far too kooky. As a psychic you are

aware that most people don't believe you anyway – never mind about having a guardian angel easing your path. It can be frustrating – you can see things you know to be true and genuinely you want to help people by telling them about what you see – and often people don't want to know or, worse, just think you're completely mad. I do understand that. I would have been like that, I am sure, before I got my gift.

It was seven years before I admitted publicly that Eric was there. I was almost thirty. My mother knew, of course. People in my family knew, and people who were close. But I didn't want to come across as crazy, and as soon as you start talking about hearing voices, that's exactly what you're pegged as. I think I felt embarrassed about it, to tell you the truth. I am very aware how much something like that sets you up for ridicule.

I had started doing shows – meetings really – where I would talk about my gift and give readings to members of the audience. In this particular case it was a big audience – around six hundred people – and beforehand I had been backstage with a bad case of nerves. My stomach was fluttering. I often get nervous before a show – after all, my gift is only in my power to a certain extent. If nothing comes to me, then I don't have much of a show. It saves on rehearsal time, but it is a bit nerve wracking. Even today I still get anxious that I am going to walk out, pick up the microphone and that there won't be a single spirit in the room wanting to contact a loved one, or that I won't be able to see anything about the people sitting expectantly, waiting for me to tell them about what is happening in their lives. It's never happened yet, but there is always the worry that perhaps it might.

That day was one of the first times I had ever done a big show and Eric had been talking to me, kindly, encouraging me and telling me that I could do it.

'Just go out there and be yourself,' he said. 'If you're genuine and you tell the truth, then no one can ask for more. And if you don't see anything, don't worry. You just have to take it as it comes and tell the truth.'

I thought about it for a couple of minutes and then I understood that I had been doing the wrong thing about Eric. By not telling the truth about him I was holding back something that was important. I suppose it was like being in the closet, like having a secret that was a really big part of what you were about, and not letting it out. I had been scared of the reaction I might get but now I realized it was time to tell people. So when I stepped onto the stage I picked up the microphone, introduced myself and then said, 'I'd also like to introduce you to Eric. He is my spirit guide.' I could see out of the corner of my eye, people in the wings looking horrified. I could feel them thinking, 'Oh God, don't say that. It's crazy.' But I carried on and explained what it is like to have Eric there and people accepted it. I came out and it felt great.

Everyone has a spirit guide. You might not be able to see that person, but they are on your side. You can ask them to help you get through something difficult. They can give you energy and wisdom when you need it. Your spirit guide is your silent witness.

Eric is always there. He is not right beside me all the time, but he is aware of me and will come if I call him or if he is needed. He's told me that I am part of his development as much as he is part of mine, though I feel as if I need him more than he needs me. Sometimes it seems as if he is being unhelpful but he is really just letting me find my own way. I can hear him as if he is in the room with me. It's a normal voice – not a spirit voice that sounds flat and mechanical as it comes over from the other side. It's like he is speaking right next to me in a deep, gravelly, experienced tone. He has no accent to speak of. I think it's a comforting voice. Other times it only appears in my head. Sometimes I see him and sometimes I don't. What I am aware of is a good feeling that he is around. Even if he disagrees with me I know he has my best interests at heart. And of course he's always turned out to be right.

It's Eric who has explained lots of things to me. Along the way I have had myriad questions, of course. Some of them are pretty trivial. For example, I asked him why ghosts are often portrayed wearing white – he told me that it is because of the mist and light that comes as part of an apparition. An apparition is basically energy, after all. Many spirits when you see them have some light around them, or appear through a misty haze. And often they come at night, so of course they seem light. It's more the perception of a ghost, really. Some are so solid and real that you can actually touch them. That would be a very strong manifestation but it does happen. I think that often people don't realize that what they have seen *is* a ghost. So the next time you pass someone who is completely ignoring you, probably seems dressed out of context, perhaps slightly old fashioned, don't discount the possibility that it might be a ghost. They are caught in their own time and they aren't aware of you. The first time I saw Eric there was masses of mist – it was almost foggy. I was sitting in my living room and had been able to talk to him for a while, so I asked him to show himself. I am not sure what I was expecting but it certainly wasn't the apparition that appeared in the doorway through the haze – a very elderly man in a scruffy robe. He gave me the fright of my life!

I also asked him about animals. I do see animal spirits, particularly dogs. Sometimes they bound up to their old owners to say hello. It's fairly common, in fact. I was doing a show in Glasgow and I had a pack of dogs running around the hall, stopping at different people in the audience. It was difficult to keep up.

Then there are practical questions. I used to wonder why some people can see ghosts while others can't. Eric says that in many cases it's the heightened awareness of someone being stressed out. It makes people more psychically aware. They are keyed up for it. Certainly, some of the families in *Haunted Homes* had been through very stressful situations prior to their hauntings and in part that is what made them susceptible.

Other conversations that I have with Eric are much more serious. Eric says that intention is the main thing in life. It is your intentions, your real intentions, that you will be called to account for when you pass over. Not that you'd get away in the afterlife by saying you didn't mean to do something which had caused harm. It's not as easy as that. It's just that in the afterlife all your excuses are stripped away, all your cover, and you are faced with your motivations, your character, all laid completely bare. So being honest is the main thing. I don't know anyone who doesn't have something to regret, after all. But if you put your hand up to something and are truly sorry then I believe that says a lot. On the other side you are reunited with your higher self so any excuses you've been giving yourself as 'cover' simply won't wash.

Bearing that in mind, it makes a lot of sense why some of the grumpier, nastier spirits don't want to go over. I can understand it. To be made to face what you've done, if most of it has been infused with ill will, is difficult. We're all put on earth to grow and learn, to basically become better people, however hard the lessons we have to take on in order to do that. As you cross you see clearly how you have truly been. Imagine realizing that you'd got it wrong, that you hadn't done your best and you'd had your chance and blown it. Even an inkling of something like that would be horrible, the worst sinking feeling in the world. I know I'd be pretty pissed off, and then afterwards probably devastated. Often, those ghosts have only made it to the angry stage. They are driven by their own consciousness, fuelled by anger or greed or whatever negative emotion it is that ended up on top in their spirit.

I am not sure if their negative emotions have simply stopped those spirits from crossing because they have been so bound up in their hatred or anger that they won't leave the material world. Perhaps, in some cases, when approaching their time to cross they have had a glimpse, an inkling of their Higher Self, and realized what they have done, can't bear it and turn away. I suppose it's a little like a child who has done something wrong and then doesn't want to admit it: the only way out is to have a tantrum. These are the most common trapped spirits I have come across in hauntings.

It is easy to 'diagnose' one. For example, I have found over the years that if ghosts move things around, it often means they are bad spirited. Not every time, but in most cases, it means they want to put their mark on a place and take control. They are looking for recognition. They want attention. They are kicking out.

One time I was called to a house in Derby. There was a ghost there who kept rearranging the furniture. That kind of activity is relatively rare and pretty high level. It takes a lot of energy for a spirit to cross to the material world in any form and to move things at all is quite phenomenal. The energy of the spirit world is emotion and if a ghost has very strong emotions then it will have stronger material powers. So it is one thing to have a ghost who might move a pillow, say, but it is quite another to have a ghost which might move the whole of the living room around.

The house had been split into flats and this ghost was only on one floor. This particular flat was a bit shabby. One evening the guy who lived there had come home at night, not switched on the lights, and had tripped over his living room furniture which had been placed, obstacle course fashion, in the hallway.

I knew straight away on walking into the house that this ghost had a very negative nature. She had probably been like that in life too. I could feel a sense of anger and frustration that was frantic and I felt this ghost had been a suicide – not a suicide born out of despair and desperation, but anger. She was in her late thirties, I'd say, and she had very dark eyes. She was wearing a long, dark dress, or maybe it was a smart housecoat. Her hair was scraped back into a pony tail, high up on her head, and it looked greasy. She had a look of annoyance on her face, a kind of spiteful, vindictive sneer. Her suicide had definitely been motivated by anger, I could feel it. In fact, the sense of anger was so strong that I felt ill. This ghost was furious and vengeful and she was desperate for attention. It was the same feeling you might experience being in the presence of a person who was just fuming with anger, except, as always with the spirit world, those feelings are more intense and amplified.

I found the epicentre of the haunting, the place the feeling was strongest, in the kitchen right at the back of the house. I concluded that had been where she had killed herself. I felt that she had died in the centre of the room, at a table, and I had a strong sense of suffocation but I couldn't say if she had gassed herself or if her death had been by some other method. I suppose gassing is most likely in a case like that. I walked into the kitchen and almost immediately Eric appeared and opened a portal. The ghost spun round and as she stared at Eric she looked completely outraged and didn't move, as would be more normal, towards the light on her own. Eric took her arm and guided her gently in the right direction. I remember feeling strange, because she hadn't seemed to recognize or welcome what had happened when the portal had opened, as spirits normally do. After she had gone I had a terrible headache. That spirit must have been a very intense person when she was alive. She had wanted attention, no doubt about it, wanted to impose her views on the household, to make herself heard.

While most hauntings are more along those lines (although she was an extreme and intense example), right at the other end of the spectrum some lovely ghosts get caught up in hauntings – good spirits. Before I was able to communicate with him directly, Eric had taken to moving things around my house. My mobile phone and my keys often went missing and then would turn up somewhere I had already looked for them. You couldn't be kinder spirited than Eric – he is just kindness itself.

'Why did you do that?' I asked him much later.

'To make you realize,' I suppose, he replied, without much interest. 'To make you realize that I was there.'

One time I was asked to do a vigil in a shoe repair shop in Canterbury – staying up at night and watching for ghostly activity. It was a very old building that had a long history. The staff had experienced strange phenomena – the more normal electrical disturbances, like bumps and bangs, along with some more unusual ones. For example, the work tools had been stacked up and moved around overnight, and things that were meant to be left on the worktops had been hung up on the walls.

When I turned up I could feel straight away a strong sense of someone being miserable, angry and aggressive. I could feel the ghost. I opened up to see if I could find out more and then I saw him. He was an older man wearing a brown working suit made from cheap material – the stuff overalls are made from. He looked as if he was alive around the turn of the last century, from late Victorian times, and he looked grumpy.

'This is my place,' he said. 'You should get out. Tell them to get out.'

'It's time for you to go over,' I told him. 'You're dead. This isn't your place any more.'

Often if you tell trapped spirits that they're dead they become confused, but he was so grumpy it didn't seem to bother him. One thing was sure – he didn't want to face things. Not his death or the fact he'd have to come to terms with the way he'd lived. I knew he was a butcher. I don't know how that came to me, but I just knew. I suppose I often know things like that about the living too – it's all part of the gift. Later a researcher friend of mine checked the records and right enough, the place had been a butcher's shop around 1890 or so.

'Get out of my shop,' the spirit sneered.

I had to hold him in one place so that Eric could take him over. I knew this might be difficult since he was clearly unwilling so I reckoned I should corner him, more or less. I started to head up the shop towards a small storeroom at the back which felt as if it would be more contained. I thought the best thing to do would be to challenge him and get him to follow me. After all, he was spoiling for a fight and it would reel him in.

'I'm just a woman,' I said. 'Are you going to frighten me, you coward? Want to get me out, do you? This isn't your shop any more.'

It worked. He began to tag along. He seemed furious. He was swearing.

Once we were in the storeroom it became a bit of a standoff. The spirit wanted me out but before we could really go at it Eric opened a portal.

'Go through,' I told the spirit. 'It's what you need to do.'

He stood there for a moment or two and then he

seemed less angry. I think he was shocked. But he didn't do as he was asked. He just stood there. Then, like the spirit of that woman in Derby, Eric laid a hand on his arm and guided him. The door closed and he was gone. I wonder what he had to face on the other side. I wonder what he had done. In any case, I hope he did what he needed to do once he got over there. If he could come to terms with his life then he'd be given another chance to make it right and by that I mean another life, another time on earth.

I do believe in reincarnation. Definitely. I believe people revisit the earth every three generations or so. Eric told me that is broadly the timescale, although it can vary in small details from person to person, experience to experience. That explanation sits comfortably with me. It feels right. It means all the family you have known will be there to welcome you on the other side, and all the family who have known you will arrive while you are over there. It is around two hundred years or so and then you come back down for your next lesson, having come to terms with your last one. I haven't seen a trapped spirit much older than about two hundred years so that holds true for me.

I like the idea of reincarnation. I believe we get a lot of chances. Those grumpy, nasty spirits aren't cast aside immediately. There is still a possibility for them to redeem themselves. They can come back down and learn another lesson. I hope they will.

Eric has shown me his place. It is the place he lived when he was alive. It is beautiful and green – a clearing in the woods that smells of grass, earth and wood smoke. There is a fire outside, some mossy logs beside it to sit on, and a building – a narrow, round, stone tower. I think it is very old. I think he lived a long time ago. I sometimes wonder where that place is now; what it is like these days. It could be in the middle of a motorway, after all. It could be a housing estate. Or a campsite. When I visited Ireland a few years ago I saw some of those towers. They are a very thin, distinctive shape with the door a floor up so you have to have a ladder to get in. I've never seen one anywhere other than Ireland, so I assume Eric must be Irish. In that last life he was an apothecary – a healer – and he worked in the woods. Eric is pure spirit now – he'll never come down to earth again. He's learning his lessons on a different plane.

When I got back from meeting the production team in London I asked Eric what he thought about the TV series. I have to say that mostly he is bored with the material world. I've asked him things before and he just sounds completely jaded and disinterested. Once I asked him why I couldn't see the lottery numbers for myself and he practically fell asleep before telling me that perhaps someone else might need the money more than me that week. Maybe he never was very material – after all he lived in a clearing in the woods and wore a dirty old monk's habit made from scratchy burlap. He looks pretty rough, really. But, then, he has the bluest eyes I think I have ever seen.

I have been offered a lot of TV work in the past but I haven't taken on much of it. Often they want you to sit there with a crystal ball looking mystical or dressed up in witch's robes. Once I was offered a psychic TV show that had to be presented in the nude – in Scandinavia, of course! Naturally, I turned that one down. I nearly ended myself with laughter when I got the phone call from a friend who was getting me bookings at the time.

'You sure you don't want to give it a go?' she teased.

'Positive,' I replied.

I think those kinds of ideas come about because most of what's sensational as a psychic, the really amazing things, can't be seen by cameras or, for that matter, by most people. So producers think they have to dress it up, I suppose, and rely on parlour tricks rather than any of the more powerful stuff. Most of the time what's on offer is gimmicky and quirky and has absolutely nothing to do with my day-to-day life or my day-to-day work. The *Haunted Homes* offer was different. It was something I believed in; these were the kind of jobs that I would take on anyway. And there was to be no fake drama and no dressing up. In fact, if anything, with all the technical equipment and a sceptical expert on the set all the time, they would be playing me down.

'This is a good way of reaching more people,' Eric said. 'And that means you might be able to help more people. Just don't lose yourself. You have to tell the truth and be genuine.'

Eric knows how tempting that is for me. It's nice to have some money. It's nice to keep journalists and TV executives happy or even to get them excited – just to give them what they want. I grew up in a family where we never had much money. I've never had a lot of money myself. And now I live with my mother, my niece and my daughter and I am the main breadwinner for all four of us.

So it's tough sometimes to turn things down when accepting them would mean that I could afford things we really want. But I try to avoid the temptation and only accept the jobs I really feel I can do well. Nothing gimmicky. Nothing sensationalist. It has to be genuine. A few times I could have taken on the jobs that would have earned me a lot of money and made me a big name. But then, that wouldn't have been real for me. I'd have had to lie or to pretend. No matter what, I have to stick with the truth.

'So you think this is a good one?' I pressed him.

'Just be real,' Eric said, 'and you won't go far wrong.'

I was daydreaming ... imagine if we got something on film: something that proved it; evidence that would reach a lot of people. That could be very important. It's not that I am stuck on proving that I am right. Sometimes when you meet people who have experienced the spirit world, whether they have been haunted or not, it really bothers them that other people don't believe what they are saying. Later on, every single one of the families in *Haunted Homes* would mention that was a problem for them to some degree or another. For me it's nothing like that. For my own peace of mind I don't need anyone else to believe what I've seen. I know it myself and that's enough. But if there is something there, then it proves there is more to life than what you can get out of it in material terms and it has to affect the way you choose to live. I wanted to do the show to try and get some of that proof because that could be a wake-up call for someone who needs it. That would be a help. I hope that over time there will be a lot less angry, confused spirits who don't want to cross over because they can't face the way that they've lived. I'd like things to get better. I'd like to see more people living good lives.

Then the door went. It was my mother coming home. We went into the kitchen to have a cup of tea and a chat.

'Looks like that TV show might go ahead,' I told her. 'They want to shoot a pilot episode.'

'That's great, love,' she said.

Mum has always accepted what I wanted to do. She has always accepted my gift. At first she was more accepting of it than I was. She calmed me down a lot when I was freaked out. I caught sight of myself in the mirror as I sat down at the table and curled my fingers around a warm mug of tea.

'Right then,' I said, thinking aloud, 'I guess I had better get a haircut if I am going to be on the telly.'

'Good idea,' said Mum. 'What do you fancy getting done?'

I just knew that this conversation wasn't for Eric. Poor guy. And sure enough all sense of him being around immediately disappeared ...

Chapter One

**The Outram Family's House. Birmingham.
Cleared on 14th July 2004.**

*The Outrams have been living in their house for several years
and paranormal activity has steadily increased over that time.
The phenomena they have experienced include orbs, inexplicable noises (bumping, banging and footsteps), shadows, movement of objects and the opening and closing of doors with no
rational explanation. A workman has refused to return to the
house because of his experiences in the attic. Several family
members have been touched and, on one occasion, hit hard by
a door swinging open inexplicably.*

The Spirit Is Built to Survive

Everything was ready to go ahead. Sam had made all the arrangements and the production team had been working hard. They had placed an advert in the national press to find families with paranormal problems at home. It was only a tiny ad – almost a listing – but Sam said there had been a huge response and it had taken weeks for the team to sort through the enormous pile of applications. I wasn't even allowed into the office! I really was not going to know anything before I turned up at the house. That was no problem for me – I had enough on my plate, I reckoned. There's always plenty of work for me to do.

I had already had a busy summer. While the production team were vetting hauntings up and down the country, I was just getting on. I borrowed a friend's flat in Sheerness for a few weeks to give me somewhere to work from – I always have writing to do. Before I got down to it, though, I wanted the place to look nice, so I sorted out some help and painted the flat to freshen it up, and then I had some new carpet laid. I figured that I was all set for a few weeks in a place where the phone wouldn't always be ringing. I love Sheerness in the summer – the cool breeze from the sea and the countryside so vibrant and green. The world seems such a different place when the weather is warm. I go for long walks in the countryside and sit outside the pub watching the world go by. Summertime is right up my street.

And then one Friday I went and tripped on a step. It was only a six-inch step, but I was in agony. I was whimpering with pain. My niece, Francesca, took me to hospital in a taxi and the x-ray showed that bones in my foot, ankle and leg were broken and the major tendon on top of my foot was severed. It was excruciating and I would have to walk with crutches for months to come.

'I don't believe it! What is this going to look like on telly?' I complained to my daughter, who tried to convince me that it didn't matter.

'It's your gift they're after, Mum. Just be glad you didn't break that!'

The *Haunted Homes* series wasn't my first appearance on TV but before, I had always been sitting on a sofa, just chatting. Now I should be moving around on camera, walking confidently from room to room, ghost hunting, and instead I would be hobbling about, leaning on a stick, unable to negotiate even the stairs on my own.

'Walking with a stick is never sexy,' my friend, Sara, laughed at me when we went out for ice cream on the Monday before I was due to start filming. It was a hot summer's day and the bandages around my foot and ankle were uncomfortable. I was taking loads of painkillers. Originally we had planned to go for a walk – a bit of a hike, really. Now we were going to stay in Sheerness. 'People watching', Sara calls it.

'This is going to look awful on the screen,' I moaned as I licked my ice cream cone, but I knew I just had to swallow my vanity and grit my teeth. Everything was ready. Sam had done a sterling job of planning the pilot and I was not going to let her down.

I was due to be picked up the next day. Apart from my foot I was a little bit nervous, I suppose. No one had told me where I would be going – not even an indication of which city the house was in, never mind what might actually be there when I pitched up. The film crew and researchers were sworn to secrecy and everyone had kept their word. Usually, of course, when people ring for help I have at least some idea of what I am getting myself into. In fact, sometimes it's impossible to stop people from talking once they start telling me their story. That night I didn't sleep much – my leg was really uncomfortable and I was curious about what it would be like working with the TV crew and, of course, what might be in the house once I got there.

In the morning Sam picked me up from home – there was no way I could make the train with my foot in that state.

'Holy Moly!' she said when she saw me. 'Are you OK to do this?'

I nodded and tried to manoeuvre myself into the front of the car, which took ages. Everything took ages in this condition. I was even drinking less tea because it was such a hassle to get the kettle on. I was hoping that I might lose weight just because I couldn't be bothered to snack between meals. It was all too much effort.

Sam remained tight lipped about where we were going, but filled me in completely on the subject of the rules while we were driving northwards, away from town. This would be the first TV show of its kind on terrestrial television and OFCOM – the TV and radio regulating authority – were monitoring it rigidly. They have some very stringent rules, even for evening viewing, and as this was the pilot it was very important that we complied with everything they wanted.

Sam had obviously been thinking about how to put this to me. We hadn't discussed anything like this before. She carefully stressed that absolutely everything had to be balanced and nothing could go out that might scare anyone. This seemed strange on a programme about ghosts, but those were the rules and if anything happened we needed to have a rational explanation for it, not only a paranormal one. I shifted around in my seat, trying to see if I could get my leg more comfortable.

I had met Chris French, the Professor of Parapsychology they had brought in as a sceptic voice, a while ago. As Sam chatted about his role, she mentioned that he edited a magazine called *The Skeptic*. I had seen the magazine before, but hadn't been aware of his connection with it. From what I had read in *The Skeptic,* I could tell that Chris wasn't only sceptical about the spirit world; he was sceptical about everything from alternative health practices to UFOs.

'I guess that would make him the Voice of Reason,' I joked.

Sam didn't believe in ghosts or the spirit world and I could see she was a bit nervous that I might have a problem with Chris's presence.

'It's only fair,' she said.

'Why don't we just see what happens?' I said. 'I think this is going to be great. And having a sceptic around doesn't bother me at all.'

I knew that the odds of us finding something that couldn't be explained away were slight. You can always find a reason, even if it isn't exactly likely. There's always the possibility of something other than the paranormal – grounds for the temperature to suddenly plummet or electrical activity to be set off. The things I see and hear, figures and voices, have never been recorded clearly. Although some interesting photographs and recordings exist, there has never been anything definitive on the record. Generally I don't think it works like that, though I wish it did. But I had high hopes that maybe, maybe, during this series there would be something strong enough to make the point.

'I don't think we're going to be able to prove things one way or another,' said Sam, oozing rationality and clearly hoping for good TV no matter what.

I could only hope. And besides, the team were rooting for lots of ghostly phenomena which would make really great TV. We all wanted the pilot to be great so that ITV would commission a whole series. I wasn't worried – I had a good feeling that it was going to be OK.

In the end, Sam and I were so keen to get to the house that we drove to Birmingham with only one break. At least now I knew which city the house was in.

Sam booked us into our hotel while I painstakingly extracted myself from the car and struggled to my room. My foot was seriously hurting and it was also badly swollen. I could hardly manage to put the kettle on to make a long-awaited cup of tea. In the end I had to sit on the floor and shuffle across the carpet on my bum, and then haul myself up onto the work surface to plug in the kettle. This wasn't very dignified, I laughed to myself, but at least I'd get a cup of tea. Sam knocked on my door to tell me that the crew had already done some filming in the house and they had interviewed the family about what had been going on. The technical team would arrive later to take readings and Chris was going to interview the family and have a look around only after I had gone in.

'So I get the first look then,' I said.

'Yes. Let's go. They are ready for you now,' she said. Sam rang ahead to tell the film crew that we were on our way, and she dropped me off at the end of the street in a nice neighbourhood near the Tyburn Road. She told me the number of the house so that I could approach by myself and see what I felt at first sight. The film crew were already set up so they could get shots of me arriving. I hauled myself out of the front seat and balanced myself with the stick.

'This might take a while,' I said to Sam.

'Good luck,' she replied as she patiently waited for me to get out and steady myself properly before she drove on ahead to park the car. As the car disappeared I looked around. It was a pretty normal, suburban street. The weather was sunny, hot for July, and there were kids' toys in the front gardens and bikes propped up at a couple of the doors. The houses were brick; some of them were painted white. It was a pretty place, which gave me a good feeling.

'Well here I go,' I thought to myself.

As I limped towards the house, leaning on my stick, I started to get a strange feeling, which got stronger as I approached the garden gate. This feeling was emanating from the house. It was something heavy and unpleasant – an air of sadness. I caught a wave of it and concentrated. It didn't feel good. I looked up and the film crew gave me the thumbs up. They had set up in the garden next door to get some shots of me arriving.

'Just ignore us,' one of them shouted over.

The house was semi-detached, but I knew already which side the feeling was emanating from. Sometimes it is that definite. I didn't have to look at the house number, I knew that I had come to the right place. The sceptical researchers had done their job. Without any doubt there was something there.

I made my way up the path and was about to ring the doorbell when a fresh-faced young girl came running up to me from amongst the film crew. She was carrying a clipboard.

'Please can we get you walking up the path again?' she asked cheerily. 'You keep pulling funny faces.'

My foot was killing me. I was supposed to have crutches, but I had refused. If I was going to be on telly the most I wanted to be seen with was a stick. Now I was beginning to wonder if the support from one stick was enough. It was getting very painful.

'I can give it a go,' I offered, hobbling back down the path, leaning on her arm.

If you look carefully at that pilot, my face looks completely frozen as I walk through the garden gate. I didn't want to let the pain show again, but trust me, it was agony.

Inside the house I met Liz and Chris Outram for the first time. They seemed like a solid couple, very devoted to each other and their family. They had been together for ten years and had four kids. Their sixteen-year-old niece, Kirsty, was also living in the house – Liz's sister was ill and they were helping out. Kirsty's boyfriend seemed to be staying as well, but he didn't like the idea of being on TV.

First off, I asked them if I could go around the house on my own. I wanted to see for myself what was there before speaking in detail to anyone living in the house. You never know what you might find and there is no saying that the bad energy I was feeling was a ghost. Someone who is severely depressed might cause that kind of energy. Someone ill-natured and grumpy might give out something similar. I'm a sponge and I will pick up on whatever is there, from the living world or the dead. If there is a teenager in the house (and here there were two) they can sometimes be the source of 'paranormal' problems. Teenagers can have a lot of manic energy around them. Sometimes they are psychic themselves and their gift is only just 'switching on'. I didn't pick that up from Kirsty or her boyfriend but they were the right age for it to happen and I didn't want to misdiagnose things – I preferred to get a really good feel for the place before getting into conversation with anyone.

As I walked further into the hallway the feeling was getting quite strong, but I knew I was not at the centre of the haunting. The house as a whole from outside felt just as bad. This wasn't where the problem was based. I hopped along for a bit. The film crew were following me as I moved around and I was aware of the pressure to say something, but I knew I couldn't just make something up as I didn't really know what was there yet.

I never make things up, even if it would help people. Sometimes it's heart rending because someone might have come miles to see me. Often, if people have been bereaved they are desperate. But if there's nothing there, then there's nothing there. The ground floor of the Outrams' house had the same general feeling as I had picked up outside the house – heavy and unhappy for sure. Something was wrong in this house but I still couldn't tell quite what it was.

'I need to go further in,' I said. 'I don't know anything yet.'

Sometimes things come to me as a certainty. I have a visual image in my mind, or I simply know something has happened. As I carried on down the hallway it hit me that there had been banging on the door and the wall, and that footsteps had been heard marching up and down. No question of it. This was a spirit, I concluded. It was definitely a ghost. It felt like a spirit had been there and I was already getting a feel for what the spirit was like. This couldn't be someone who had died young. It had a feeling of bitterness and heaviness that only comes with older age.

'Well,' I thought to myself, 'at least any teens in the house are off the hook. There is definitely a spirit here.'

While I was sensing things in the hallway we heard a bell sounding upstairs. The family said that it wasn't one of their alarm clocks. It wasn't a noise they recognized – they hadn't heard it before.

One of the crew ran upstairs and returned with the news that the sound was coming from the attic. Steve and Helen, who were part of the crew, grabbed a camera and went upstairs alone to investigate, leaving me with a camera running downstairs and one other crew member. I couldn't move quickly enough to follow them, as stairs were so difficult for me. And besides, I preferred to work my way through the rooms methodically and really feel what had been going on.

There were no windows in the attic and the light switch was inside the room itself, so Steve and Helen had to climb the stairs to the attic in the dark. The bell was going off and then on again and they scrambled about for a torch to see what they could find. No one could figure out what was making the noise. As it turned out they couldn't find any evidence of the bell's source. It kept sounding and then cutting out. We could hear it downstairs.

'Weird,' someone commented as we waited for them to come back down.

It was broad daylight and the Outrams had had most of their experiences at night time. I think that the spirit knew I was coming and had set off the alarm. I think that when I sensed it, even when I was approaching the house, it sensed me too.

'Here I am,' it was saying. 'I am upstairs.'

Meantime I was still hobbling around at the bottom of the house when Steve and Helen came back down, shrugging their shoulders and saying that they couldn't find a thing. The bell had stopped now anyway. I decided it was time to go up towards the bedrooms. As I slowly made my way up the stairs the feeling of paranormal activity got stronger. I was heading towards it; I could feel the draw. On the first floor the worst sensation was in one of the kids' rooms. I sat down on the bed and the film crew perched around me. I had the sense of something intense and miserable and I knew how awful it must have been to live in that atmosphere. Right at that moment there wasn't even a spirit in the room, but it had been there and I could sense it. I felt desperately sorry for the family. It doesn't matter if you believe in ghosts or not, whether or not you can pick things up directly, something like that is so oppressive that often someone living with it might feel depressed and not know why.

I felt strongly that this had been going on for a long time. Children had been woken up in this room and there had been noises. It felt embedded in the atmosphere. I knew that whatever was there had made the people who lived in this house very unhappy. Later the family confirmed that three of their four kids had tried to sleep in that room and had all been woken in the night. Toys had disappeared or been moved around in there too, on a regular basis.

I kept moving on. Past the bedrooms there was a door opening onto the steep, internal stairs which led to the attic. Liz was hovering at the end of the hallway, checking how I was doing.

'The cat won't go anywhere near that attic,' she commented, but didn't say anything more. She disappeared back downstairs as I opened the door to the concealed stairway. It was difficult to climb with my foot so stiff and sore, but I made my way up on my knees, taking the stairs one by one and balancing carefully as I rounded the sharp bend into the room. There were a lot of household goods piled up against the walls, stored in boxes and covered over with old sheets and lace tablecloths. There was an open space in the centre of the room. I knew immediately that the attic was at the epicentre of this haunting. The feeling up there was stronger than it had been anywhere else. My heart was pounding.

'This is where it is coming from,' I said. I could feel that it was an old man. The experience of knowing things in a situation like that is physical as well as psychic. I was shaking slightly. I could feel the energy hitting me and then an image popped into my head; an image of the man as he was in life. It was only there for a moment and then it disappeared. I held onto the essence of that image. I could feel it. I had a sense of him. I knew that he was bossy and very strong-willed. I think in life he wasn't a pleasant person. From experience I knew he probably didn't even know he was dead. He was one of those confused spirits who are bound up with strong emotions. If hate or rage fuelled him in his life, it would still be with him. More than anything I think that he was domineering and officious. I felt light-headed and for the first time I was glad that I had a stick to lean on. 'I mustn't switch on too far,' I thought. It was like having a radio on low – just enough psychic sense to know there was a spirit there. Not so much as to get involved too quickly. I wasn't to clear the house until the next day.

It took a while to get downstairs again, though going down the stairs was easier than going up them. As we passed the bathroom Kirsty was in the hall and told me that she had seen the shower curtain move. 'It really moves,' she said. 'And sometimes the doorbell just goes for no reason. That's happened lots of times. It really freaks me out.' The whole family were clearly very jumpy and anxious, and having felt what was there I could hardly blame them. I was probably the first person they had spoken to who had experience of this kind of thing and they were keen to hear what I had to say.

I decided it would be best if we all went back downstairs.

I ended up on the sofa in the living room. The oldest of the Outrams' four kids was ten and that is far too young to be included in what we were doing, so the production crew had arranged for them to be taken care of elsewhere for the day. More than anything we didn't want to frighten the children, and all along that had been Liz and Chris's main concern, so they hadn't told the kids anything about their fears. I had a lot of respect for Liz and Chris for doing this. I see it quite often. When people are afraid they tend to just blurt things out, and Liz and Chris had restrained themselves admirably. The Outram kids just thought they had been waking up in the night because of strange dreams or because it was cold and the duvet had slipped off the bed. They knew their parents had been a bit jumpy of course, but they didn't know anything specific. That is absolutely the right thing to do if you have younger kids. It can scare them for the rest of their lives if you let it slip. Kids have such vivid imaginations.

Sixteen-year-old Kirsty, who had joined us on the sofas, was old enough to know what was going on and why there was suddenly a psychic and a film crew knocking around the house. Chris said that for a long time he hadn't wanted to believe anything paranormal was in the house but he had taken some footage up in the attic with a video camera and orbs of light could be seen moving around the space up there.

'That was it. That was when I really knew,' he said.

Chris had also seen a candle flicker and extinguish for a moment or two before lighting itself again.

'These are all signs of paranormal activity and I am not surprised you managed to film something up in the attic. That is where the centre of the haunting is located,' I said.

'So there is a spirit?' asked Chris.

'Yes. Definitely.'

'And it's up in the attic?'

'That's the centre of the activity. The epicentre of the haunting. The spirit can move all over the house, though.'

'I'm not surprised it's up there,' Liz said.

As it turned out Liz had refused to go up into the attic for some time. She had had too many frightening experiences up there. Only a few weeks before the film crew arrived there had been a builder working at the top of the house.

'That builder,' Liz told me, 'was six feet tall. He was a huge bloke you'd never have thought would be scared of anything. After an hour he came tearing down the stairs because something had touched him and he'd heard scratching. We had wanted to take down the panels in the attic and open it all out. We thought that might help. Now I am scared of what might be behind those panels. The builder said he'd do anything we liked from the outside, but he didn't want to come into the house again.'

'Yeah,' said Kirsty. 'Tell Mia about the door.'

Chris said that the door to the attic had swung open for no reason on two occasions. Once it hit Liz in the face and on the other occasion it hit Kirsty's boyfriend with such force that it gave him a black eye. But the door was always kept locked ...

'I've heard a growling noise up there too,' said Liz. 'It's horrible. And I often hear things moving around as if heavy furniture is being dragged about.'

'Once again, these are signs of paranormal activity,' I said. 'I can see you have been having a very tough time.'

So far I had only been listening to the Outrams, but it was time to open myself up to the energy in the room. I wanted to see if there were any other factors. It is always best to quickly read the people who are living with the haunting. I found myself focusing on Liz. She hadn't been speaking any more than the others but I was drawn to her. I was surprised. Usually it is the teenagers, like I said before. But in this case Liz's spirit shone like a beacon. She was nervous, I could feel that, and also very good natured. I liked her. She had bright red hair and sparkling blue eyes, and I knew she was naturally confident; someone who was normally happy and fun to be around. Despite this, she, I realized, had had the worst time of it. As I focused on her I began to understand why.

Some people do feel the spirit world more than others. Some people are susceptible. In Liz's case I could see that she had something in her past; a strange relationship with her father which had left her vulnerable and sensitive to these kinds of experiences. I don't want to say too much about Liz's private life. Later, I spent a lot of time with her while I was in the house and I promised not to disclose our discussions. I never break a confidence if I give someone my word. It is enough to say that her father was dead – he passed over years ago. But Liz had never come to terms with her life with him and she was a sensitive person; someone open to feeling things. As I sat on the sofa taking in the atmosphere around her, there was no doubt in my mind that she had had far more, and far worse experiences than anyone else in the family, despite the fact that she wasn't actually talking about them. It was obvious that she was more open to it.

'What about you, Liz?'

Liz ran her fingers through her spiky hair and took a breath.

'One of the first things,' she said, 'was when I heard a baby crying one night. I rushed upstairs to check the kids, but they were all asleep. And then the crying just stopped. I can hear something in the house a lot of the time. It growls. And sometimes it moves things. One of the pictures in the living room, that one over there, flew off the wall last week. And I have seen strange shadows. Shadows that don't make any sense because they couldn't come from a light nearby. I saw one disappearing through the attic door. I hate it up there. Sometimes I get so scared I go and sit in the garden until Chris comes home. I don't like being here by myself. We can't be a normal family any more.'

I realized it was time for me to tell them what I knew so far. I wanted to tell her why she had been so personally affected; why she had been vulnerable.

'Well, the house is definitely haunted. But there is something I am sensing from you, Liz. There is an older man who is now in spirit and who has had an effect on you.'

I was set to carry on, to tell them everything, but as soon as I said that Liz jumped up off the sofa in a blind panic, burst into tears and, with her hand over her mouth, bolted out of the room and into the kitchen.

Everything stopped. I was so sorry. I knew that I could help this family. I knew a spirit like the one in this house could be sent to where it belonged and that the problems could be over in just a few minutes. I didn't want to upset Liz – that wasn't my intention. I like to think that I am very careful with people. I always try to put things as gently as I can. But sometimes you have to tell someone something, and they have to know it. I wanted Liz and Chris to understand what had been going on and that had to include all the reasons for it. In my experience, when people don't understand they will only scare themselves silly, even after the ghost is gone.

Psychic clearing isn't like any other domestic problem. If the plumber says he's sorted out your piping, you believe him. You don't spend the weeks afterwards waiting for the pipes to block up, dreading the moment that something springs a leak. But if you're working with ghosts you have to show people, tell them what's going on when you are sending a trapped spirit over to the other side and then, ultimately, they feel a lot more secure. If you don't, they are still anxious as hell after the ghost is gone and that only causes them more problems.

Before we sat down I had decided not to tell the Outrams just how heavy the spirit felt. They didn't need to know that kind of detail. It was a definite, strong, unpleasant presence – one of the strongest I had ever felt. But I did know that they had to understand what it was and why it was there. After all, it was a semi-detached house and the people on the other side of the wall had had no trouble at all. The ghost had been drawn to the Outrams. More specifically, the ghost had been drawn to Liz because of the emotional spectrum she had. It was really all about her and what had happened as she was growing up. She had to understand that because it was an honest explanation. And most importantly, I really felt that both Liz and Chris would have to be there when the ghost passed over because after a couple of minutes the whole place would feel different. If you feel that change happening, then you know that the spirit is gone. For someone as sensitive as Liz that would be very important because she would be able to trust what had happened and then, afterwards, she wouldn't be afraid.

Liz, however, had disappeared in tears before I had even started. I looked at the space she had left on the sofa, then Chris jumped up and followed her out and they went into the back garden to have a chat.

Kirsty and I joined them in the garden, and they told me that Liz's father had been a very dominating personality. In fact, Chris told me that as soon as I had said there was an older man in spirit, Liz's father had sprung into his mind as well. He put his arm around his wife to comfort her. I went back into the living room with Kirsty. Liz's experiences with her father had obviously been very traumatic and even ten years after his death she still hadn't come to terms with their relationship. Kirsty shifted uncomfortably around on the sofa. I felt so sorry for everyone – they had been through such a lot and I desperately wanted to help.

'I didn't mean to hurt her,' I apologized to Kirsty. 'Ask your auntie if she wants a word with me on my own. If we can clear this thing then it'll all be over. It can be finished if we just sort it out.'

In the end Liz and I chatted for ages. She told me that she had been terrified that the ghost was her father and I realized that my explanation had convinced her of it. I have to be careful all the time. I have to make sure that I am clear in everything I say. I don't want anyone unduly upset. Anyway, I was able to reassure Liz on that score. The spirit I could feel was from a long time ago. He had been dead far longer than her father and although he was connected to the house itself, or rather, the land on which the house was built, he wasn't connected to the family in any way.

'It is only that your relationship with your father has drawn this spirit out and made it easier for him to manifest. The spirit world is about emotions and in the spirit world you can't hide them. I promise it's going to be a lot better,' I said. 'I won't leave this house until the spirit is gone. I'm not going anywhere. After this there will no longer be anything you can't speak about.'

Later on that afternoon the technical team arrived and set up their equipment. The production team had arranged for Ghost UK to take readings. Ghost UK is a company which deals with measuring paranormal activity, and they had a lot of specialist equipment with them. In general they don't work in private houses. David, who runs the company, seemed very nervous. He hadn't been on television before and spent ages practising what he was going to say. On the other hand, his assistant, Mark, was more relaxed.

David and Mark both had a more technical approach to the subject. They didn't believe in ghosts one way or another; they just measured whatever they could – temperatures, electromagnetic fields and footage from infrared cameras, as well as using sound recordings and movement sensors. Their usual method is to record something unusual and, if they can, to find a rational explanation for it. Sometimes power lines overhead cause high electrical readings, or noises can be traced to defective piping. These were the experts who should be able to corroborate my findings.

David and Mark set up equipment all over the Outrams' house. By the end of the afternoon most of the rooms were rigged with movement sensors, sound recording equipment and infrared cameras. A round of temperature readings was taken, all pretty constant at around twenty-four degrees, and David also took readings of the electromagnetic fields in the house. He had never seen such high electrical readings at a property of this size. In particular it was unusual because the readings didn't fluctuate very much – the equipment was consistently reading at an elevated level which peaked in the attic.

When I saw something in the corner of one of the rooms I asked David to take a reading.

'Over there,' I said.

He rushed over with a black box in his hand.

'Wow. A lot of electrical activity over there,' he said, making a note.

'This is great,' I smiled. 'You can measure what I can see. No one has ever done that before. I feel like I can prove something here.'

I was really beginning to enjoy this. I know when I meet people sometimes they might see my eyes wandering off because I have noticed something paranormal. Now I felt I could at least have some proof that I have not been staring at thin air.

The top of the house was definitely the hot spot, no doubt about it. While David was checking the equipment he felt sure that he saw something move. He only glimpsed it out of the corner of his eye but he was positive that there had been a movement. Mark didn't like the attic at all and said that he felt light-headed and unwell after being up there.

'It's spooky anyway, isn't it?' he said. 'No windows.'

'The attic was boarded up when we moved in,' said Chris, who had followed us up. 'We opened it. And that bit over there – we were going to open that up behind those boards. But now we won't. It might get worse, mightn't it?'

Mark and David set off downstairs to double check the rest of their equipment, and found that the movement sensor they had set up in one of the children's bedrooms had recorded something. A toy from the dolls' house had moved right across the floor by itself and landed in the middle of the sensor's sweep. There was no one in that room when it happened, although David was just outside the door. I could see that although he was nervous of the cameras he was also eager to find out about what was going on.

Once everything was in place Liz announced that she had made a big pot of tea, so we all went out into the garden. The atmosphere changed immediately. It's difficult to be nervous when it's lovely and sunny and there are lots of people about, so it was reassuring for the crew and the technical team. My foot was still aching and I was glad to sit down again, and one of the crew brought me a small table to rest my leg on. I was dying for a cigarette and lit one immediately. I realized that this could be a long night.

Sam was sitting next to me checking things off on a list attached to a clipboard.

'So far, so good,' she said.

'Still sceptical?'

'Open minded,' she replied with a smile.

Off in the distance the doorbell rang and someone went to answer it. A moment later, Chris the sceptic came into the garden and said hello to everyone. He was given a mug of tea and Sam asked him how he wanted to proceed. They needed to get some footage of him going over the list of occurrences and making his assessment. I was definitely not needed so I settled down in my chair and relished feeling the warmth of the sun on my face. I had big plans for staying in the garden.

Chris the sceptic went inside with Liz and Chris and interviewed them in the living room, checking for a history of drink and drug abuse, psychiatric drugs or nervous disorders to no avail. Liz told him that she had tried to find a rational explanation for all the activity there had been in the house, but eventually there were just too many abnormal events to be explained away, and there were so many things for which she simply couldn't find a rational explanation in any case. Chris took copious notes, but did his job and remained completely sceptical.

Now the whole team was in place and once things were all set for the evening, we organized some food and the Outrams left to stay elsewhere. The plan was for the crew and paranormal team to stake out the house without the family and see what we could find. At midnight we were all in the living room, drawing straws for where we were to be stationed. Sam wanted to have people keeping watch in every room in the house and decided that it was only fair that everyone should rotate their position on an hourly basis. It would keep us all awake and divide the hot spot between different people so that no one would be sitting in the epicentre all night while someone else was dozing away in a room where there was no activity. As it turned out, no one wanted to have to sit up in the attic, especially not on their own, so Sam had to send up two of the guys together, leaving one of the kids' rooms empty.

When you watch film which has been made using infrared equipment it looks as if it's actually light; as if anyone being filmed should be able to see. For the avoidance of doubt, let me tell you that's the scientific genius of it. You'd be lucky to see your hand in front of your face. So there we were, one person to a room in most cases, in a haunted house in Birmingham, sitting completely in the dark, just waiting. I was lucky that I just don't get scared, which is odd in a way. I mean, I was the one who believed. And yet, some of the sceptics were bricking it.

One of the cameramen was a real hard nut. He'd worked with a war correspondent for a long time and didn't scare easily. Those guys have often seen awful things – they are in danger, in the thick of the action, and often put themselves in harm's way for the sake of good footage. It's part of the job. Anyway, he was up in one of the bedrooms with another crew member and they shouted that they had something on film. Everyone rushed downstairs as if there was a fire. It was really exciting.

'Oh my God. Oh my God,' one of the researchers was saying.

'Shhh,' Sam soothed her.

Behind us the cameraman came down holding his equipment ahead of him as if it was a precious object, looking as if he was in shock.

'There's something up there. We saw it. We got it on film,' he said quietly, the sound engineer behind him nodding. He set the camera down on the table.

The room was silent as everyone got to work. One of the crew rigged up a monitor to play the footage. Everyone crowded around the table to see the tiny screen.

'I'm glad the lights are on in here,' joked Sam.

A couple of people smiled nervously as the cameraman fast forwarded through the tape, concentrating to find the right piece of footage. Beside me Helen was flexing her fingers out and in with the tension.

'It's here,' he announced, and the video started to play.

The images on the screen were scary, pale green and slightly out of focus. In the corner of one of the bedrooms a hooded figure with a skeletal face appeared suddenly and then faded out. The skull was shifting its gaze from left to right, as if it was looking around. There was only a suggestion of it, a half glimpse, even on film. But it was definitely there. A being, cowled and almost translucent. The cameraman froze the frame.

'There,' he said.

No one seemed able to say a thing. We were all staring at the screen. Then someone behind me said, 'I want out of here now.' Chris the sceptic was standing next to me staring at the monitor, just shaking his head in disbelief. He looked really shocked.

Sam was looking around the room nervously. She was looking paler than usual, her eyes lighting on the monitor and then zooming off to the corner of the room. I realized that she was trying to figure out if it might have followed us down, but I knew that the apparition wasn't in the room.

'It's all right for that lot,' I thought to myself, 'but I am the one who has to go up there and face it.'

I felt more confused than anything. It didn't make sense. Skeletons don't walk around and ghosts don't appear as skeletons. I had never seen it before and yet, here it was. I watched them play the tape again and tried to figure out what was going on.

All I could come up with was that this spectre was meant to scare us. That in this house there was a ghost that wanted to scare people and, well, a skeleton in a cowled robe had certainly achieved that. From the moment that I first arrived at the house, I had felt that this ghost was very, very heavy. My mind was racing ahead. I wondered what it was going to take to get something like that to go over to the spirit world. It was confusing me because most paranormal activity has a function. The bumps and the bangs are meant to get your attention or to vent an emotion. I hadn't ever met a ghost that actually just wanted to frighten people. Often spirits do things that are scary, but that isn't their intention. So this was strange. I hadn't seen anything like this before and I couldn't figure out why a ghost might manifest itself in that way.

'I feel sick,' said Helen, rubbing her stomach. 'What does it want?'

Then the cameraman started to giggle. He had a real naughty boy look on his face as he pointed his finger at the monitor, shaking his head.

'Gotcha,' he said.

Sam rounded on him. 'You did not plant that?' She sounded threatening.

But they had. It turned out that the two of them had cut something in from a horror movie and transposed it over their film of the bedroom. It had had us all fooled.

Sam went nuts. I think she might have fired them, but we needed a crew and it was after midnight. Instead, she called them everything from irresponsible to sadistic, tore a few strips off them and proceeded to give a lecture about how it was important to be serious on a show like this. A ripple of relief ran through everyone in the room, including me. We were all glad it was a practical joke, truth be told. Chris the sceptic stood there with a big grin on his face as one of the crew went back and played the shot over and over again, this time to everyone laughing.

'Very realistic,' I said.

The cameraman was looking slightly shamefaced after Sam had finished with him. 'This happens again, and people will be fired,' Sam said. 'We can't have this kind of thing. No more practical jokes.'

'Sorry,' he mumbled.

I suppose she was right.

Then it was time for us all to get started again. Whatever had happened, I could still feel a presence in the house. A real one. We headed back to our posts – with Sam insisting that the cameraman and his mate go up into the attic by way of punishment. The two of them were stationed up there for some time, and right enough it was in the attic that the first incident occurred another couple of hours in. It wasn't as dramatic as the hooded spectre, but both of the guys felt their ears pop and an eerie sensation, like a pressure drop. One of them said that he could feel a constriction in his arms and legs and the other felt his heart beating very fast. That always happens to me too when I am in the presence of a spirit. It's a physical reaction over which I have no control. Chris the sceptic went upstairs and suggested that it might be from the electromagnetic field. Perhaps there was just a lot of electricity in the house.

A few minutes later the temperature readings in the attic started to rise very fast, even though the place felt freezing. David went up to monitor them and very quickly the readings had reached the same temperature as a hot summer's day, although you wouldn't have wanted to be in the room without a jacket. It was freezing up there. The last reading taken was over thirty degrees and that rise (which was several degrees) took place in about two minutes. There was no logical explanation. It just didn't make sense.

Sam was standing in the hallway and saw some shadows she couldn't explain in the children's bedroom. A soft toy had fallen, inexplicably, to the floor. This time Mark from Ghost UK went in to investigate. He replaced the toy and tried to get it to move by jumping up and down. Perhaps some kind of vibrations had made the toy take a tumble. He jumped around for a bit but the toy stayed put. Mark cursed under his breath – there wasn't a camera set up in that room so he wouldn't be able to figure out how it had really happened. There seemed no reason for the toy to fall just by chance. The Outrams had reported toys being moved on a regular basis and here we were, missing the opportunity to gather evidence when it happened.

For a while it went quiet and then the assistant producer and the director saw something moving under a blanket that had been thrown over a chair. Chris the sceptic arrived on the scene again and said that perhaps what they had seen was caused by lights outside. Perhaps a car had gone past and they had seen the headlights moving across the room. An optical illusion.

'Could be,' mused the assistant producer, though she didn't sound convinced. It is difficult to tell what's paranormal and what's rational if you can't really see and sense things like I can. Put a few adults in a house, tell them it's haunted and make them sit up all night and, well, someone is bound to think they've seen something. But then there was also a bank of technical evidence mounting up and some of it couldn't just be explained away. Chris couldn't come up with any explanation for the temperature fluctuations in the attic. They were too dramatic to be natural, and there was no heating equipment up there; nothing that could generate that kind of heat so quickly.

By five in the morning, when it was getting light outside, everyone was spooked and pretty exhausted. We packed up the cameras and headed back to the hotel to get some sleep.

'How do you think we're doing on proof, then?' I asked the sceptic.

He smiled at me. 'I'm not saying there isn't something going on. I just don't think it's paranormal. I don't think it's a ghost. I don't believe in ghosts.'

'But you do think that something is in there. Something is going on even if we don't agree on what it is?' I pushed him.

And he had to concede on that. 'There will be a rational explanation,' he insisted, although I don't think he ever came up with one that explained everything that was going on in the Outrams' place.

After being up all night, my foot felt as if it had been run over. I crawled into bed, falling asleep straight away, and when I woke up the aching had gone. I don't usually stay up all night. Most times I do a spirit clearance it happens in the day time. It was really for the cameras that we had to try and get some evidence of the haunting. I had spoken to Sam about it ages ago, about how we were going to try to catch something on film. I said that it had to be at night. This wasn't only for the atmosphere (though that works really well), but in general, spirits are most active at night. Ghosts are a form of energy – that's why the electromagnetic readings were showing so high in the Outrams' house. Very late at night there is less human electrical activity to interfere with spirits. It's not that there isn't spirit activity in the daytime – it's only that they have a clearer hand to the world late at night and it's easier for them to get through. Studies show that it's between 1 am and 4 am that most activity is reported. That's just the way it works. If it's dark it's easier to see orbs, for example, or even a very dim apparition, which wouldn't be clearly visible during the day.

I see ghosts at all times of the day and night. It doesn't make much difference to me – it can happen any time at all. I can be out for a pub lunch with a friend and meet a ghost on the way to the loo. That's happened a few times. I saw my first ever ghost in the daytime. I was a teenager, before my gift was even switched on. I was coming down a flight of stairs with a friend and we both saw a young boy fall ahead of us, crash down the stairs violently and then disappear at the bottom. It wasn't a trapped spirit, or anything like that. The boy's spirit had gone over to the spirit world. What we saw was only an imprint, a memory. We did some library research at the time and it turned out that fifty years before, to the day, that boy had fallen and died, exactly where we had seen him. He was dressed in smart clothes that placed him in the right period – posh clothes, I called them. But what we saw wasn't a ghost who could interact with the world. Not the kind of spirit who was in the Outrams' house – someone who was trapped. The little boy was only an image, like a time loop. His soul had passed over and wasn't there any more. It was just like watching a video replaying.

The majority of ghosts I see aren't imprints and, to be honest, they aren't trapped spirits either. The ghosts I see at the shows I do or during my everyday life are, in the main, visitors. They are spirits that have passed over and have only come to visit the people or places that they knew in life. I believe they are only allowed to come if it won't hold back the people they visit from their own lives. For example, when someone's partner dies, if the survivor saw their spirit, even a year or two afterwards, it would stop them moving on. That isn't fair. That doesn't happen. Most spirits can't return within two or three years anyway. They need to acclimatize to what has happened. It was years before I saw my brother – years before that could be allowed.

In the afternoon, back in Birmingham, once we were all refreshed we gathered in the hotel lobby and headed back to the house for the second night of filming. Liz and Chris met us there, keen to see what had happened the night before. The kids were sleeping over with friends. We told them about our vigil, showed them the temperature and electrical readings and filled them in on what everyone saw and felt. It seemed affirming for them, I think, that other people had experienced what they had been living with all this time. Most people who have a ghost in the house are a bit embarrassed to talk about it, and it's unlikely, if they tell their friends and family what has been going on, that they will get a positive reaction. Now, after years of strange experiences, the Outrams were suddenly faced with a group of people who had seen and felt it too. Even the sceptic said something strange was going on, regardless of whether he believed it was due to a ghost. Liz had an air of relief about her.

Later that night I would be clearing the spirit. To clear a spirit it is best to go to the epicentre of the haunting and so we had to do the clearance in the attic, where the feeling was strongest. Because electricity can interfere with spirits I didn't want any lights on. The crew set up some tea-light candles on the floor so that we could see and Liz, who hadn't been up to the attic in a long, long time, promised to overcome her fears and get herself to the top of the house to witness the spirit leaving. I had to admire Liz for taking that on. She was so sensitive that the haunting had been worse for her than for anyone else in the family and she was being very brave.

Deliberately, I hadn't opened up to the ghost fully until that evening. I knew that if I opened up completely the ghost would be called to me. After all, he was looking for attention and here I was, attuned enough to see him. Spirits always know if you are sensitive to them. One time I was out for a meal with friends and a ghost wanted my attention but I was busy enjoying myself, so I just ignored her. She came over and hit me hard on the shoulder. It almost knocked me off my chair. She had chosen to come and get me – not anyone else in the restaurant – just me. She wanted my attention – wanted to cross over. Eric came and opened a portal and over she went, and I went back to enjoying my evening in peace. Ghosts can sense the gift and are drawn to it, just, I suppose, as I am drawn to them.

In the Outrams' house so far I had sensed what I could without opening up totally, but I had intentionally not gone any further. I had held back. I was the only person who didn't see or hear anything strange the night before. Up in the attic I sat on the floor to one side of the candles while Liz and Chris sat on the other side. The film crew were all huddled up, uncomfortably, at the other end of the room. I don't get bothered by cameras, thank goodness, but it was still strange to do this while they were filming. I knew that there wouldn't be much to see – certainly nothing a camera could pick up. All they were likely to film was me sitting there, mumbling to myself, helping the ghost over. And while the place would feel different very soon afterwards, I knew that it wasn't going to come over on camera. In fact, most of the people there weren't going to be able to feel the difference at all.

'People are really going to reckon I am mad now,' I thought to myself. 'I can't believe that I am doing this on telly. Oh, what the hell!'

I took a few deep breaths and moved myself into The Zone so that I could work. Going into The Zone is like letting yourself go limp and being completely accepting of everything around you. It's a meditative state, I suppose, a place of complete detachment, which is the key. As soon as you start to relate to what is going on, you can't pick up psychic information any more.

As soon as I achieved that state, I saw an old man. He was right there in front of me, on the other side of the Outrams. He was in his fifties or sixties and his hair was light grey, almost white. He was wearing dark, heavy work trousers, a collarless shirt and a jacket with thin lapels. He looked quite rough, his eyes were dark and hard, and he had an unpleasant expression on his face as if he was sneering at me.

The ghost spoke directly to me. When spirits speak it's not with their original, human voices – they sound curiously flat, almost like an electric voice box, and almost completely monotonal and expressionless. The spirit said he had been in charge of people, collecting money in the area. He had been respected – or feared. This was definitely the ghost I had felt before – someone bossy and domineering, still wanting to leave his stamp on the people around him. He was also rather conceited – although he didn't look particularly wealthy or important. I think he had inflated his own value and role, and I had the sense of him being quite arrogant. With the manifestation of his spirit, as my grasp of him grew, came a sense of what this place had been like when he was alive. A place with water, a stone building, maybe a chapel, and lots of open, green fields. I also sensed that hangings took place nearby.

I'm not sure this spirit could even see the house as it really was: the Outrams' home. Spirits live on in their own memories. Their world is not material any more, it is emotional. All the things that you don't see, they can. If you are angry, a spirit will see that before they even notice the chair you are sitting on, for example. Sometimes they won't notice the chair at all. That old man probably flickered between the place as he knew it and the place as it was. Being trapped must have been confusing. Most trapped spirits I meet do seem befuddled.

Then, the ghost appeared to settle down. The air about him softened slightly. I think he was suddenly contrite. He apologized for some writing on a wall: something that had caused arguments and was his fault. And he said something about children's toys being moved. Later Liz explained this to me. When she had her nieces and nephews to stay there had been unexplained graffiti on the wall downstairs – too high for the kids to have done.

It had caused fights and in the end she and Chris had just painted it over. Children's toys had been moved out of the attic recently, prior to the workman arriving – the workman who ran away. It is strange what sticks in a spirit's memory. These were the things he had seen and that he wanted to tell me before he passed over.

After the ghost had finished, Eric, my spirit guide, appeared beside me and opened a portal to the spirit world. The light flooded into the attic. To me, the ghost had felt so bad that I thought he might resist leaving but he was no trouble at all when it finally came to it. The man walked right past Liz, across the candles as if they weren't even there, past me and over into the light. It only took seconds and he was gone. The portal closed and Eric disappeared, while all the time I was saying a prayer, De Profundis, which Eric had suggested I learn years ago. De Profundis is a Latin psalm, which I took some time learning to pronounce. I always use it when a spirit is passing over.

'It feels different in here now,' Liz said. 'This is going to take a bit of getting used to.'

We decided to sit up in the attic for a while just to let the feeling of the spirit being gone settle in. After a few minutes the crew switched off the cameras. There was a feeling of shock for Liz and Chris, now that it was all over. It had been a long journey for them – they had lived with this spirit for years and now they had their house back. Everyone was laughing and chatting. Often after a clearing I notice people seem slightly high. There is a feeling of elation that makes you want to laugh.

'Would anyone be an absolute angel and make me a cup of tea?' I asked. It was going to take me at least ten minutes to make it down the stairs and I preferred to stay in the attic for a while anyway, but I was parched, gasping.

After we had finished filming, Sam arranged for the production team to do some research to qualify what I had sensed. It turned out that the area around the Outrams' house was open fields two hundred years ago, and that there was a hanging place nearby, up on the Tyburn Road. There was also a stream that would have passed right under the house but which was diverted some years before. There was no record of the stone building I had sensed, which I felt was a chapel of some kind. However, it did turn out that the area had been a centre for the Catholic community, though no record remained of where they had worshipped.

The camera crew went back to Birmingham a couple of weeks later to check how things were going since the ghost had been cleared. It was nice to see the footage of the family looking much more relaxed, playing games together and just very much back to normal. They had experienced no more paranormal activity in the house – all the electrical appliances were working properly, everyone was sleeping better and the strange noises, orb lights, moving objects and shadows had stopped. The ghost was gone. As for the crying child, I believe that this was one of the visitors I mentioned earlier, and nothing for the family to worry about. I had a few calls from Liz and we talked about her family – she still rings me from time to time when she has some news or just for a chat.

I went back to Sheerness and got on with my life as usual. The programme wasn't due to air until the winter so there was a long wait to see if ITV would want to go ahead and commission a whole series. I kept in touch with Sam, nipping up and down to see her. My foot had now mended completely and it was a relief to be able to walk normally again. We went to Soho House and did some star spotting. Most of the time, though, I was at home. I kept myself busy.

I had set up a website and was trying to look after it myself – I got a lot of mail and I found it was impossible for me to keep up with the amount that was coming in. If you send me an email please don't think I don't care, or haven't bothered to read it. I try to sift through what arrives in my inbox but I can't answer everything. I decided early on to prioritize people who have a dead child or someone missing because that is the core of my work, the heart of what I do. Often, by the time I've written one email back, having really thought about what to say and got it right, ten or twenty more emails have arrived.

Meantime I waited to hear about *Haunted Homes*. The pilot episode with the Outrams ran on television over the Christmas holidays and there were no complaints, or rather, just one complaint from a viewer who said that it wasn't spooky enough! In fact, there were lots of nice comments about the show and it seemed to go down really well. I went to London to meet Sam. She had watched the episode a million times and had decided to make some changes to the format if she got the commission for the series. The house would be sealed overnight so there was less chance of sabotage or outside influence. No more practical jokes. A diagram would come up on screen to show exactly where paranormal activity had been sensed to make it easier for viewers to keep track of what was going on. Last of all, the family (or the adults in any case) would be able to stay in the house on the night we recorded so that we could get their reactions. We were just waiting for ITV to say yes.

It felt like it was taking ages. Then one afternoon Sam called me from Los Angeles, where she was working for a few weeks on another project. Sam is unfailingly glamorous.

'We got it,' she whooped. 'We'll be filming six episodes this summer.'

It was already May.

'When?' I asked.

Sam thought for a moment. 'August. We'll be filming for around a month so clear your diary, Mia.'

Six spirit clearances in a month. That was more spirit clearing than I normally did in six months. And Sam's team would be picking out difficult ghosts – those were the ones with the most dramatic stories, the ones that caused the problems. I lit up a cigarette and took a deep breath.

'Right,' I said. 'I'm up for it. That's great.'

Chapter Two

**The Scriven Family's House. Birmingham.
Cleared on 13th August 2005.**

The Scrivens have been living in their house for over twenty years and paranormal activity has steadily increased over that time. The phenomena they have experienced include orbs, inexplicable noises (bumping, banging and footsteps), sticky stuff appearing overnight on mirrors and movement of objects. Twice, people have been pushed in the upstairs hallway and have fallen down the stairs. A friend working in the house has refused to return because of his experiences in one of the bedrooms. A child's footprints were discovered on some wet varnish that had been left overnight. Members of the family have felt cold spots and have been touched at night time. In a family photograph taken in the living room there is the clear image of a sinister, dark figure.

We Leave an Imprint Wherever We Go

By the time we were ready to film the whole series my foot was a lot better and I only had the odd twinge now and again. I had a busy time in the run up to August and though I was excited about the filming it was good to keep busy. I got the train to Birmingham New Street where Claire, one of the production team, came to pick me up. New to the team, she was a young, perky girl who seemed very cheerful, waiting on the concourse when I got off the train. It was a gorgeous, sunny day and by the time I arrived it was lunchtime, but I had grabbed a sandwich on the train and wasn't hungry.

'That's great,' said Claire, 'because we want to take you to do the psychometry right now.'

This was one of Sam's new ideas for the series. She had made a couple of changes in the way things were to run. Psychometry is the ability to pick up information from objects. I have had this ability for a long time; in fact, it was one of the first psychic talents I realized I had. In the past, for example, I have been able to tell if a person is alive or dead by simply looking at a photograph of them. If the person is dead then their eyes look 'flat' to me. It is as if the eyes are vacant. I have had parents come to me with pictures of their missing kids. It feels like a huge responsibility when that happens, but I always try to be truthful. One time a couple came for a reading with a picture of their daughter who had been on a beach holiday in Asia when the Tsunami struck. They were convinced their daughter was alive and had brought a photograph of her to their reading in the hope that I might be able to help locate her. I held the photograph and concentrated for a moment.

'I'm sorry,' I said, 'your daughter has passed over.'

The couple went crazy and started shouting at me. I can't blame them. But I also felt I had to tell the truth and there didn't seem to be any more gentle way to put it. They were in uproar and stormed out of the reading, saying that they were definitely going to find the girl and that she was alive, no doubt about it. They said they could 'feel' her. Later I learnt that the girl's body had been found and I had a long telephone conversation with her mother, which I hope helped in her grief.

It's not only photographs that I can read. Any personal object can also be tuned into psychically. Any object can be used, although personal items that are treasured such as jewellery or watches often give the strongest readings. Sam had arranged to take a few articles from each haunted home before we started filming, to see what I could pick up. In the car on our way from the station Claire told me the objects from the Scrivens' house were waiting, laid out in a hotel room. As we pulled into the car park I realized that this wasn't the hotel we were staying in – it was much too posh! I think they wanted a room that looked very smart as a background for the session. Anyway, the idea was that I would do this before meeting the family or visiting the house to see if I could pick up information about the haunting simply from the family's possessions. I knew there would be some 'stings' set up for me. They might put out old-looking photos of people who were alive, for example, to see if I might read that they were dead. That was fair enough, I supposed. I was there to be tested.

When we got to the hotel room there was a table set out with about ten articles on it. There was a pottery clown, several photographs, a white stuffed dog with red glitter paws, a brown bear, two watches, a ring and a fine gold chain. I sat down at the table and waited for the nod from the camera crew before I picked up anything. I wanted there to be no doubt that I hadn't been tampering with the items or chatting to anyone about them before the camera started rolling.

'Right,' said Claire. 'Ready?'

I took a moment. 'Yes,' I said, and I moved into The Zone.

First I picked up the clown and I felt that this ornament had been involved in paranormal activity – it had been moved by a spirit from wherever it normally sat. Then I touched the larger of the two watches and was overcome with a feeling of intense rage. I had a sense that a family had been fractured and split apart. Around the white toy dog there was a feeling of someone holding onto it, being afraid and crying. The two strongest readings came from the gold chain and one of the photographs, of an elderly lady. The lady, I felt, was a visitor now. She had been dead for some years and I had a strong sensation of love around her – a sense that she was a kind-hearted person who was committed to her family. She wasn't haunting the house, but I knew that she visited there to see the people she loved. It made me smile because my feeling about her was that she was good natured and love-ly and I got a very positive sensation from just holding her photograph. When I picked up the gold chain I knew it had had two female owners and had been passed down from one generation to the next. It had been a gift, given in celebration of a relationship.

'That's all I get,' I told the crew, one of whom had been scribbling away frantically as I was speaking. No one gave any indication if what I said had hit the mark, and they began to dismantle the camera and pack everything away. I have to say, it is odd not to get a reaction. People usually confirm what I have picked up in the reading and the crew had clearly been briefed not to give anything away. It didn't bother me, but it was very different from doing a private reading. I nipped out into the sunshine while I was waiting for them to pack up their kit. Next we would be going to the house.

By the time we left the hotel it was well into the after-noon and the sky had clouded over. The place felt muggy and heavy as it was still warm despite the clouds. We drove for what felt like ages to get to a place called Northfield. We were very close to the Longbridge Rover Plant which had closed earlier in the summer, and as we passed the site it seemed strange that such a large factory space was clearly empty with no one around. It was totally deserted, and such a sad sight.

The car pulled off the main road and down a couple of side streets, and we stopped around the corner from the house where the team had parked their big, black Winnebago. This enormous motor home had been specially hired for the series and was wired so that every part of the haunted house could be monitored from outside. This was another of Sam's changes – she had decided it would be best to 'lock down' each house while we were inside, allowing only the family, me and the two other experts, Mark and Chris, inside. The night vision cameras would be static and the crew wouldn't be allowed in unless they were called for help.

After we had said hello to everyone and Claire had organized a big pot of tea, I was introduced to Vanessa, our pretty make up girl, who worked miracles on my face and hair while I sipped away at my tea and indulged in a chocolate biscuit or two. We had a laugh and she asked me to tell her fortune. I saw her being romantically involved with a DJ – I hope it's now come true for her.

The Winnebago was amazing – it had a fridge which Claire had ensured was full to capacity with snacks to keep everyone going, colourful bench seating with enough room for the entire crew as well as a shower, a toilet and enough storage for the cameras, monitors and sound equipment. I immediately felt at home! The seats were comfortable and everyone was smiling.

Claire and another of the production team, Gemma, ensured that everyone was ready, and I checked myself in the mirror (Vanessa had done a grand job), took a deep breath and then walked round the corner towards the first haunted home in the series …

My initial impression was what an ordinary street it seemed. The houses were terraced, each with a small front garden and driveway. The flowers were in bloom because it was high summer and I could hear that somewhere nearby someone was mowing their lawn. Kids were playing out in the street and there was the sound of laughter and chatting floating on the air. It was a really nice place. Gemma had told me which house belonged to the Scrivens and the idea was that I should go in alone and look around by myself before meeting the family. As I approached the row of houses a small circle of kids noticed the cameras and started standing around to see what was going on. Off to one side I could see them pointing and giggling. However, as I got close to the terrace I forgot about the kids staring, and about being filmed, and concentrated on scanning the row of houses to see what I might pick up. Immediately it felt as if the Scrivens' house was staring back at me with wide, black eyes.

'That'll be the one, then,' I thought.

There was a lovely hanging basket at the door, but even walking up the path the atmosphere already felt heavy. As I stepped through the front door the house felt oppressive straight away. The place itself was beautifully kept: the paintwork immaculate and brightly coloured, and everything neat, tidy and clean. There were sunflowers on the dining room table and the sun was shining in through the net curtains and into the living room.

Nonetheless, it didn't feel like a happy home. Psychically, I picked up a real sense of discord. There had obviously been big problems. I knew that noises had been heard in the front room and I also felt that orbs had been seen. The atmosphere in the dining room (open to the living room) was particularly bad. I had an unpleasant sensation of discomfort, like slightly heavy air pressure. I moved into the kitchen but I didn't pick up any strong sensations there – only that the kitchen drawers had been rattled by some paranormal activity.

I found myself drawn back out into the hallway. Here it was a different story. The sense on the stairs was harsh – my heart rate began to climb and I felt goose bumps coming up on my skin. I had all the physical sensations of being afraid without actually feeling any fear. So far this seemed like the most intense place in the house, paranormally speaking. I knew this ghost was a man. I had a sense of him being emotionally very, very heavy. I thought the stairs were probably the epicentre of this haunting. Some terrible things had happened here. I had an image of someone falling down the stairs and I wondered if they might have died. Things had definitely been seen here and already I felt that the temperature around that area was lower than in the other rooms.

I decided to keep going and climbed up towards the bedrooms, and on the upstairs landing I was able to confirm that the area around the stairs was the epicentre of this haunting. Although I could tell that people had been scared in all three of the bedrooms – someone had been touched in bed and there had been sightings of an apparition – the atmosphere up there was much lighter than on the stairs themselves. I was shocked to find that there was no child's room upstairs – I felt that was somehow missing. I had a strong image of a child's bedroom, but I had no idea why.

'It's all going on around the stairwell in any case,' I said to the camera. 'That's the centre of it. It is spilling out into the other rooms, but the stairs are the centre.'

At this point I had to close off my senses as I didn't want to contact the spirit yet. I had seen enough for now. This had been a terrible haunting and I felt angry that the people who lived here had had to put up with such a heavy presence. I was already protective of them. This spirit just shouldn't have been there.

Downstairs, the crew invited the Scrivens back into the house and I got to meet them in the living room. Lorraine, the mother of the family, was divorced. She had short blonde hair and a mischievous smile. I could see that she was the power holding her family together – she had a very strong spirit. Her two grown-up children, Stephen and Emma, had clearly been rattled by the haunting and both of them seemed nervy. Emma was petite and pretty and had amazing, wide eyes. Stephen seemed very energetic, as if he was about to jump up and start running around at any moment. He had a wide grin and told me that he was intending to join the police force. I immediately saw that they were sensitive people and that this had been particularly hard on them.

'Hello,' I said as I reached out my hand. 'I'm Mia.'

When I told the Scrivens what I had sensed so far they agreed with my analysis. The stairs had been the centre of activity for some time. I discovered that they had lived in the house for almost twenty years, but that the last four years had been overtaken by this haunting.

'At first I thought it was the ghost of a child,' Lorraine said. 'I found some children's footprints on newly-painted varnish downstairs a few years ago. That didn't bother me. But lately it has been much more scary.'

I wondered if that was why I had felt there should be a child's room upstairs, but I didn't tell the Scrivens about it. That child was most likely only a visitor. It is very rare that children are 'left behind'.

Meanwhile, Emma told me that she had seen an apparition. Recently she had swapped bedrooms with her brother because he was having such dreadful nightmares. In the bedroom Emma didn't experience any bad dreams herself, only this visitation.

'It was a man and he appeared beside my bed. His face looked really badly decomposed,' she said, rattling off the story at me.

'She was screaming to the point of hysteria,' Lorraine confirmed.

'There is no way I am going back into that bedroom,' Emma said.

In fact, Emma was so afraid that she had been sleeping with her mother ever since and hadn't so much as gone back into her own bedroom since the night of the incident. She didn't like being in the house on her own any more and had been timing her schedule so that there was always someone else around when she was at home.

'I go all cold,' she said. 'And I didn't like the look of that thing. I hate the look of it.'

'Don't worry,' I explained to her. 'Sometimes as apparitions gather their energies they piece themselves together and they can seem deformed. It probably never got together properly. I don't think he had a rotten face. I doubt what you've seen is evil – it just wants to establish its presence.'

I hoped that this comforted her. I didn't want to scare the family or freak them out, but the feelings in their house were very, very strong. And I already knew that this was one of the strongest spirits I had ever had to deal with. It was crossing my mind that perhaps it was an evil entity. I couldn't feel that yet, but there was certainly a very strong, dreadful atmosphere in the house. On a scale of one to ten in paranormal activity, I was currently placing this haunting at about six or seven, and I'd only just started investigating it. That was high and potentially dangerous. I had to keep my eyes open and not rule out any possibility. It was my job to keep everyone safe. This thing could not be left here.

Then Lorraine told me that when she was decorating in the hallway her ladder shook and she fell down the stairs. A family friend, Steve, had been decorating in the house previously and had a similar experience. He felt his head being pressed hard and then he had the sensation of being pushed over. Another friend had been painting one of the upstairs bedrooms and got so spooked that he now refused to come back into the house at all.

'I think you have been fortunate,' I said. 'I speculated earlier that someone had fallen down the stairs and maybe died. You have been very lucky.'

Stephen told me that one morning when he came downstairs there were smears of a sticky substance on the mirror.

'It was really difficult to clean off,' Emma confirmed.

Unfortunately, I had no idea what that substance could have been, and later, the other experts were confounded by this report too. It was a great shame that we didn't have any of it to send to the laboratory.

On top of all these other paranormal problems that the Scrivens had been suffering, Stephen had been taking photographs in the living room one evening. When he downloaded one of the images onto his computer there was the shadowy figure of a dark man in the corner of the dining room mirror.

'That was when it hit home, maybe there is something in the house. Maybe it's real,' he mused.

Later, Mark from Ghost UK put this image onto his computer. He couldn't figure out how it had been generated. Chris, the sceptic, was disbelieving as usual and wanted to try to recreate the conditions in the photograph to see if we could cast a large, man-shaped shadow in the corner of the mirror. We never did that but as Mark said, when the photo was taken there had been people in the living room to witness any irregularities, and for the figure to come up large and dark, right on the sofa, where it was shown – well, it didn't seem possible that it was a shadow or a trick of the light. He pronounced it 'a good photograph'. I knew that photographs of paranormal activity are rare, and seeing the photograph that Stephen had taken only added to my sense that this haunting was very serious.

'I'm desperate to get this sorted,' Lorraine chipped in. 'Seeing that black figure. It's sinister looking. It's really unnerved me. It's capable of doing a lot more.'

'Don't worry,' I said. I felt outraged. This was a terrible imposition – this spirit had been going from room to room scaring the life out of this family. I admired Lorraine for her strength of character and I felt sorry for the kids. I sensed that Stephen was more affected by this than he seemed outwardly. I worried for him because he had a lot to deal with in this situation and I hoped that he would get over it. As for Emma, she had had a very rough time too, but I sensed a strong connection between her and the kindly lady I saw in the photograph when I was doing the psychometry. Now this lady appeared behind Emma and told me that she had been having a very hard time – things had been really tough emotionally, and a lot of that was to do with relationships.

'You've been lost in your own way, haven't you? But now things will be lighter. I promise. You're going to have some fun,' I reassured her.

Emma started to cry.

'Are you all right, darling?' I asked her, and she nodded bravely.

I was so angry that they had had to go through all this. How could something dare to play with such a nice family? They didn't deserve it. I wanted to reassure them.

'Don't worry,' I said, 'I'm not leaving until it's gone.'

'We'll hold you to that,' Lorraine replied, and then she gave me one of her mischievous smiles.

Later that afternoon Gemma drove me back to the hotel. I was starving and went down to the restaurant to have something to eat. Over salmon, salad and chips I gathered my thoughts. Most of all I was nervous in case this spirit did turn out to be an evil entity. I had the family to think of as well as the film crew, most of whom didn't believe in spirits at all. I hoped that whatever had been haunting the Scrivens' house was just a very bad, but human ghost.

'What do you think, Eric?' I asked.

And as always, Eric was there. 'You can handle it,' he said, confidently.

That evening I arrived back at the Winnebago and Vanessa was there again to do my makeup. I felt like a superstar! She put the final touches to my hair and make up, and then the cameraman ran a check on the night vision camera. The make up was fine, but the top I was wearing went completely see through when the lights went out and Gemma had to run around and find me a jumper to wear! The jumper had a large weave but it was the best we could do, although you could still pick up the vague outline of my bra.

'Pervy and psychic. This is some show,' one of the crew joked.

It started to get dark. While the cameramen wired the cameras in the house to a monitor outside, Claire and Gemma went out to a local takeaway and brought back a huge pile of pizzas. Everyone dug in with gusto. Some of them had such hot chilli on top that it made my eyes water and I decided to stick to the plain ones, but they all disappeared eventually, so the chilli didn't defeat everyone. Steve, the family friend who had felt the ghost push him on the stairs, also turned up. He was going to join in, which I could tell was a big support for the family. As the pizza boxes emptied everyone was getting nervous and I noticed that one or two people had sweaty palms already.

It was late – well after eleven – by the time we settled down to do the vigil.

Lorraine had been very specific about the ghostly activity and had noticed over the years that the majority of paranormal incidents in the house took place around 3 am. We would start at midnight.

I gathered everyone in the living room to give them a pep talk while Gemma distributed torches for use once the lights had gone out.

'Please be careful,' I warned. 'It will be very dark with the lights off and the activity is around the stairs, so make sure you switch on your torches and can see where you're going, even if you get frightened. Don't worry. It can scare you but it can't really hurt you.' I did think, though, about Lorraine falling down the stairs and I realized that I would have to keep my eyes open and look out for everyone.

At midnight we were all in position. Mark and Stephen were in the hallway, by the stairs. Emma and Steve were in her bedroom (which had taken a lot of nerve as Emma hadn't been back in there since seeing the apparition). Lorraine and I were in the main bedroom – we'd agreed that Lorraine would stick to the left hand side of the bed which was where she normally slept. Everyone else was outside – Chris was monitoring us on a screen and the technical crew were finally getting to dig into their share of the pizzas.

I counted three – two – one and then the lights went off.

It took a minute for our eyes to adjust and, as before in the Outrams' house, I was amazed at the night cameras being able to pick up such clear, bright images in such inky, pitch black. It didn't take long before both Lorraine and I noticed a grey shadow by the door. It was misty, like the snow you get on a TV screen. There was a slight breeze in the room, particularly around our legs, and Lorraine said she had a pressure headache. I was fascinated – any sign of paranormal activity that I can share with another person always intrigues me. As I was not 'switched on' psychically I realized that this evening we really were experiencing the same phenomena in the same way, despite my gift. I was seeing what Lorraine saw, even if I was more intrigued than afraid of it. Lorraine, however, was petrified. 'I don't like that,' she said, as the strange shadow hovered in the doorway and became so dense that I couldn't make out the frame clearly any more. It had a strong energy and my heart rate was out of control. I decided to move towards the door and as I did so the menacing shadow disappeared. I checked out in the hallway – that no one was messing around with a torch – but the boys were downstairs and Emma and Steve were in another bedroom. The place was completely black.

Back in the bedroom I swapped places with Lorraine, who was shaking so much that the bed was moving, poor thing. We both saw the shadow again, only this time it was moving along the hallway. My heart was still pounding. Lorraine could feel it too. The shadow moved off towards Emma's room. Later it turned out that this movement was picked up as a flash of pink on the thermal imaging camera that Mark had placed at the top of the hallway. A few seconds later Emma called out. She was panting with fear and Steve was feeling ill. He had a

everyone was suffering from the effects of the pressure and temperature changes in the house. So, after less than an hour in their home the Scrivens asked to leave and we all went back out to the Winnebago.

The crew passed out chocolate biscuits and cold drinks from the fridge and the atmosphere quickly relaxed as everyone settled down into the caravan's comfortable seats. Steve was rubbing his temples as his headache eased off. Lorraine tried to explain what the headache was like.

'It's not sore, it's more a pressure,' she said. 'Like my head is being squeezed.'

After a few minutes' relaxation, we decided that the experts should go back into the house and Lorraine bravely volunteered to come with us. We decided to use her bedroom again, since that was where we actually saw the cloud-like, misty phenomenon. Chris the sceptic was game. I got the feeling he was always hoping he would see something, but it was a running joke that nothing paranormal ever happened when he was around. I felt that it was unlikely that anything would happen, because my experience is that four is too many people for any kind of shared manifestation. While I can see a ghost in a crowded pub, for example, no one shares my vision of it. It is extremely rare for more than one or two people to see the same thing. I am not sure why – but it just doesn't seem to work like that. Eric once told me that it was simply 'too much proof at once'.

We trudged inside the house and back up the stairs. Stephen and Emma were watching us on the monitor; they seemed very concerned about their mother.

'It's a step too far for Mum,' Emma had commented.

And I could see how difficult it was for Lorraine to sit back down on her bed and wait for the ghost again. Certainly what she had already experienced that night was more than the light touch on the cheek or the 'strange feeling' that she had described to me when I arrived at the house.

We sat and we sat, but we saw nothing. I didn't want to open up psychically; I wanted to experience what everyone else was feeling. There was a slight variation in light in the room, but it wasn't as dramatic as what Lorraine and I had seen before and it was easily explained away. After a while of just sitting there with the tension mounting, we went back downstairs.

'I think we all saw what we thought we would,' Chris said.

He had felt nothing, but the rest of us had noticed the slight change in light, even if it wasn't very conclusive. In a way I had to agree with him. It is very rare that a sceptic will see anything paranormal – if only because they are so determined that psychic phenomena do not exist. Mostly psychic phenomena are gentle – a slight breeze, a touch on the cheek, a thought occurring to you – all of which can be explained away easily.

It was almost 5 am, and dawn was about to break. I was too tired to argue my case. I felt completely drained, having been up all night, and I walked away from the Scrivens, promising to be back the next day. The crew were dismantling the equipment as I climbed into a car to go to the hotel. I pulled my coat around me and chatted to Sam, who was driving. We were just drawing up to the hotel entrance when I got a text on my mobile phone telling me I had walked off while still wired up to the sound system – a little black box was attached to the back of my trousers.

'God,' said Sam, 'I wonder if they've been listening to us chatting all the way home?'

'Lucky we weren't gossiping,' I joked.

I promised to keep the sound equipment safe and climbed the stairs to my room quickly – I couldn't wait to get to bed.

The next morning everyone slept in until lunchtime. We weren't due to start filming until late afternoon so once I had had a bath I rang a friend who lived nearby and we met up at a pub down the road for some lunch. I was ravenous and we piled through three courses and a nice glass of red wine each before I realized that it was already after three and I had to get back to the hotel for my lift over to the Scrivens' house.

By four or so Vanessa was doing my make up again. It felt so luxurious to have someone look after that side of things for me. I had rustled up another top – and this one, when we checked it, didn't go see through, thank goodness. The crew were mostly doing follow-up interviews with the family – the morning after the night before. Then they moved on to rigging up the cameras for the clearing. I had decided that we should do the clearing in the dining area – it was close to the stairs which, after all, were the epicentre of the haunting. The production assistants were running around with candles so that the whole room could be lit without using electricity (which interferes with spirit energy) and the director announced that he had decided that we wouldn't start until late on so that there would be no noise disturbance from the street.

Gemma arranged an Indian takeaway which we all picked at in the Winnebago until it got dark, and I chatted away to the Scrivens, who were still nervous.

'It will be gone, won't it?' Emma asked, flicking her pretty, blonde hair.

'I'm not leaving till it's gone,' I assured her. 'Don't you worry.'

But actually I was worried. It was a lot of pressure, not just to do the clearing for this family, but also having to worry about the cameras. I knew that at a clearing there isn't much to see unless, like me, you are a medium. I would have to keep a running commentary going so that the cameras would have something to film. Also, there would be a lot of people around – the director, crew, production team, the family and, of course, the other experts. I felt responsible for everyone's safety. What if I couldn't find the ghost? What if I couldn't get him to go over? Or maybe he wouldn't speak to me at all, and I would be unable to get any details about why he was in the house. I picked at the curry in front of me and tried to chat away so that no one else would know that I was nervous. It would only make them worse.

By midnight the street was silent and most of the other houses were dark. I walked along to the end of the road to gather my thoughts and then strolled back to the house. The front door was open and when I walked into the living room it was glowing with gentle light. The walls were a lovely peach colour, which picked up the luminosity of the candles beautifully. It looked gorgeous with the mixture of tiny night lights and thick-stemmed candles flickering away.

Lorraine, Stephen and Emma were already waiting, seated at the pale, oval dining room table, and I slipped in beside them, at the head.

'First,' I said, 'I am going to try to communicate with the ghost. I am going to bring him into this room. You may feel what you have felt before but nothing more than that. Expect temperature and pressure changes. Don't forget that whatever you think, this spirit can't hurt you – only scare you. I will try to talk to him and get him to answer any questions you have. Whatever happens, once I have started a clearing I don't stop. However long it goes on.'

I took a deep breath and centred myself. In the Winnebago I had still felt tired from the day before, but now I was energized. This, after all, was what I had really come here to do. Out of the corner of my eye I could see Chris, the sceptic, next door in the living room watching us. 'Right,' I thought, 'you're going to reckon this is completely ridiculous. Here I am, talking to a ghost you don't believe in. You must think I'm nuts.'

And then I saw the family, seated along the table next to me, and I realized that this was for them, really. I focussed my attention, and opened myself up psychically.

I was searching the house for the spirit. I was not physically moving, only my psychic self was on the hunt. To everyone else it looked as if I was in a trance, but in my mind I was walking around the table, out into the hall and up the stairs. As I reached the top step I came across a dark figure. The ghost was there. He had his back to me. I could sense his anger already. He was wearing a cloak, like an old-fashioned travelling one of heavy cloth. He had boots on too and a dark brown garment underneath the cloak, which I couldn't see properly. I'd say he was in his thirties or early forties. As he turned around I could see that Emma has been partly right – there was a disfigurement on his face, like old, unhealed wounds under his jaw on the left side.

'Come with me,' I said, and led him down the stairs and back into the dining room. Although I walked through the archway, the ghost came through the wall, which I later found out was exactly where there used to be a door. He moved down beside the table.

'He's in the room,' I told everyone. 'What do you want to ask him?'

The Scrivens shrugged their shoulders and I noticed Stephen looking around, and Emma wide-eyed as they tried to figure out where in the room the ghost was standing. Actually, he was stationed with his arms folded, leaning against the wall close to me. The family didn't have any questions that they could think of, so I just carried on and tried to find out some details about this ghost and this haunting. The spirit was staring at me, a slightly amused look in his eyes. I pushed forward, psychically.

'This ghost's name is Michael,' I said, as I started to pick up information. 'He is from this area – this is where he lived. I am getting a date in the range 1840 to 1860. That is when he worked on an estate near here, though he has a connection with Ireland. I can see horses, stables and a set of pistols. This isn't the only house he has visited, though it is easy for him to be here because you are so emotionally open.'

At this point, Michael started to criticize the family. He had a sneering tone and told me that Lorraine didn't do enough and that she needed to get a life, and that Emma was an 'emotional mess'.

'And the boy – he is just stupid.' The ghost sneered dismissively. He was being very abusive. It was clear to me that this man was bitter and had simply been terrorizing the Scrivens because he could – it was an amusement to him. I didn't tell anyone what he was saying.

Instead, I tried to push myself further into the spirit's consciousness, wanting to know more. I saw that he felt abandoned by his family, either because they had deserted him when he was alive or because they had died and left him behind. He was furious about that and it seemed that almost a hundred and fifty years in spirit hadn't brought him any forgiveness or understanding. I saw that his own death had been violent and sudden and, if he wasn't murdered, he was most likely a suicide. It is difficult to describe how this particular information comes to me. It is only a feeling, because mostly a ghost will not tell you that kind of thing. It is like meeting someone you know and understanding why they are behaving in a particular way. It is very intuitive.

Sometimes ghosts do talk to me, but mostly, at the Scrivens' house, I saw images of this man. The dates came to me in figure form, and I could see the estate where he had worked. There was a chestnut brown horse in a wooden-doored stable. He was a very powerful presence and I could feel myself starting to shake.

Beside me, Eric arrived, appearing to my right.

'I am going to send the ghost over,' I announced, and a doorway of light appeared.

But Michael did not want to leave. As he approached the door he suddenly sidestepped and came striding towards me as if he meant to get hold of my spirit. I felt sure that he wanted more. He was after something; trying to gain some advantage over me; trying to manipulate me as he had done the Scriven family. He was furious and frustrated, and I could so easily understand how he had created such a menacing presence in the house.

Then there was a shift in the atmosphere and he began to back off, slipping away from me. This had never happened before. Usually spirits go over pretty easily – they realize that it is the right thing for them to do. I started battling with him, trying to psychically pull him back and impose my will on him. It took a few minutes, and beside me I could hear the Scrivens shift in their seats. Eventually, though, I managed to compel him back towards the portal. It felt very intense and there was a strong sense of hate in the air. My heart was pounding and I had difficulty breathing.

'You are going over,' I thought, determined. I could see this was going to be a struggle. I knew I just had to hold my ground. For some reason Michael was reticent about going into the light. He started to move very slowly, with Eric beside him. 'I mustn't break my concentration,' I thought, and I concentrated hard on my breathing. Slowly, slowly he approached the doorway and then at last he went over.

I said the De Profundis prayer that Eric had taught me, aware that Chris probably knew how to recite Latin much better than me and hoping I pronounced it all right. As I opened my eyes I was shaking, not with fear, but out of the intensity and the effort.

'He didn't want to go over,' I explained. 'And look at me. I never shake.'

Then I spread my arms out because already the room felt so much better, and said, 'Gone. You'll sleep better tonight. All done.'

Afterwards we stayed in the house for a while. The family had bought gift bags for us.

'Surprise,' beamed Lorraine, as she handed out the presents.

In my bag there was a bottle of vodka with a sweet note that read: 'Exchanging one spirit for another'. Claire and Gemma were given boxes of chocolates for looking after the Scrivens' dogs while the filming was going on.

We were all in a good mood and the house felt light and clear again. The crew began to dismantle the cameras and I slumped down on the sofa, chatting away until about two in the morning. Emma told me that she had done some research on the local area and that there had been, for some time, a leper hospital nearby. I wondered if the disfiguration under Michael's chin was in fact leprosy – maybe that was why he had been abandoned by his family. Poor guy.

When we finally got back to the hotel, I went straight to bed, but found myself just lying there, running over everything in my mind. I had difficulty settling down to sleep despite having been up most of the night, two nights in a row. I was annoyed by the imposition of such an angry, unpleasant spirit on such a lovely family and I couldn't get things straight in my mind. It was as if Michael's anger was rubbing off on me. I really wanted to know more details of what really happened to him in his life. Very late, I called for Eric and asked him why it had been so difficult for me this time.

'He is only a troubled spirit,' Eric said. 'Very troubled.'

'I hope that Michael's family were waiting for him when he crossed over and they had a chance at last to resolve their feelings for each other,' I said, because that was worrying me, too.

Eric gave nothing away, though he was reassuring.

'There's nothing wrong,' he said. 'Get some rest, Mia. Let it go.'

In the end, I saw dawn breaking through the curtains before I finally settled down, and managed to miss breakfast again because I was sleeping so deeply. As I drifted off to sleep I wondered where we would be off to next. I only had a couple of days back at home before the next house. 'Maybe,' I thought, 'the next one will be easier.'

Chapter Three

The Harris Family's House. Huthwaite, Nottinghamshire. Cleared on 26th August 2005.

The Harrises have been living in their house for over a year and have experienced paranormal phenomena during most of that time. These phenomena include orbs, inexplicable noises (bumping and banging), movement of objects (a picture was turned upside down on the wall) and a man's voice heard over the baby monitor in the children's room, talking to one of the children. Every member of the family suffers from nausea, headaches and a more general feeling of discomfort. On two occasions four-year-old Carly Beth has been pushed down the stairs. Carly Beth has also complained of 'friends' coming to visit her and has said she doesn't like these friends any more and wishes they would go away.

It's a Gift – You Have to Open it

In the end, September were having difficulties with the schedule so after the Scrivens' house I had more than a week off before I had to go to the next location. I spent a lot of that week in London with Sam. It was sunny and we lolled around on the swing seat in her leafy back garden, chatting, only occasionally rushing into the kitchen and getting ice cream out of the freezer to cool ourselves down. On a couple of the days I made appointments with some private clients and apart from that I spent a bit of time on my own, wandering around Kew Gardens. The break gave me time to think.

It is genuinely very rare for ghosts to be as heavy as the one I had sent over the week before in Birmingham. Now I realized that the likelihood was that all the ghosts in the series would be extreme cases like that. After all, you don't want to ask people into your home with a camera crew in tow unless you really have a problem. And for me, those heavy cases are draining. Psychic energy is like physical energy – if you do too much it is tiring. I have never been sent anything to deal with that I didn't have the resources to handle (even if it was afterwards that I realized that fact). Nonetheless, it was daunting. I had five more houses to visit and I couldn't help wondering what might be in store for me, and what kind of shape I would be in by the end.

When the arrangements had been made Sam gave me a train ticket for Sutton in Ashfield. I got out the road map and had a look – it was right off the M1 in Nottinghamshire.

'We're packing you off up North,' Sam joked, a twinkle in her blue eyes, and as ever, she didn't say any more about the house or the haunting. I had to go in blind.

Sam wasn't coming with me this time – she had work to do in London. She said she might come up and visit me on set, though. I hugged her goodbye at the station and found myself a quiet seat on the train. Gemma was going to pick me up at the other end. I bought a Diet Coke and a ham sandwich from the trolley and stared out of the window as London disappeared slowly, the buildings tailing off as we headed northwards and the green fields and rolling landscape taking over.

Gemma was standing on the platform grinning as I got off the train. It was early afternoon and she had a hire car waiting. The sun was beating down.

'You're off to do the psychometry first again,' Gemma said.

'Another posh hotel?' I asked.

'No – this time we've hired a room in a business centre. I spent all morning making it look atmospheric.'

'Great. Lead on,' I said, hauling my bag into the boot of the car.

Gemma drove through a couple of pretty villages that looked almost like picture postcards, until we pulled up at a modern building. Some of the film crew were sitting outside smoking, waiting for us. It was nice to see them all again after the break.

Inside, Gemma had done a great job and the room looked full of character. There were bookshelves and a desk so that it looked almost like a private library in someone's house. She lit a couple of candles to finish off the effect.

'Well done,' I whispered to her and gave her the thumbs up.

The cameras were almost ready and I checked myself in the mirror while the crew finalized the lighting. The table had been laid out already with the possessions of the family I was going to visit, but some of the items were larger than we'd had before and were propped up at the side. I wondered what I might feel from them.

When the director said that he was ready I sat down and looked at the items one by one. The largest was a child's dolls' house, made of plastic – it was mostly white, blue and pink, and it was hinged to open in the middle so you could play with dolls and furniture in the tiny rooms inside. The toy house, I felt, had been bashed about and had a very negative atmosphere around it. As soon as I touched it I had an overwhelming feeling of blinding anger that seemed completely out of place with a child's toy. It took me aback, I have to say. This wasn't a childish fury – a temper tantrum – it was a malicious, adult feeling of intense hatred and anger.

Next, I moved on to the other large item – a print in a gilded frame. The picture was a rural scene with horses and fields and children playing. I was hit immediately by a strong sense of misery. This picture had been in an atmosphere of very intense unhappiness and I could pick up that emotion very strongly. I was sorry for the family in this house already.

From the table I picked up a gold ring and knew there had been a lot of tears in the wearer's life and that people who cared about each other had been pulled apart. Next there was a child's toy – a cloth rabbit with a concertina tummy and a pull string to make it play a tune. I had the feeling that this toy had been operating on its own – that the tune had played at random – and I also felt that whatever was in the house had been scaring the children. There was a strong sense of that.

I moved on to an ornament – a china box with teddy bears and books inside – and as soon as I touched it I knew it had been thrown. Again there was a feeling of anger around this object. These items were worrying me. This was a ghost that wanted the family out. There was no question in my mind that the spirit in the house was furious and worst of all it had definitely been having a bad effect on the children in the family.

'It's very worrying,' I explained on camera. 'I can't believe that whatever is in the house is interfering with the children. That just isn't on.'

I already felt very defensive of the family, just from

touching these objects. I could feel that they had had a very tough time and this ghost seemed heavy already. In particular, the anger, although it came to me in flashes, was very strong. I also had a strong sense of a doorway being important, but I didn't know what that meant.

'This is going to be a big one,' I said to Gemma as we left the room, and she nodded silently, but didn't tell me any more. Later, it turned out that Gemma had been the person who had gone up to interview the family before they were accepted to appear on the programme. She said it was the first time that she had ever felt a presence herself. It had been the middle of the day and Gemma had heard inexplicable banging while she was interviewing the family in the house.

'I had that cold feeling that other people describe,' she told me later. 'I felt it was surrounding the entire outline of my body and it gave me goosebumps. I have never experienced anything like it before and was completely freaked out!'

After the psychometry, though, Gemma maintained the ban on telling me anything in advance and she didn't say a word. September were very good about that – not letting me have any information at all. I know people think when you're filming a TV programme like *Haunted Homes* that things are staged. I can put my hand on my heart and honestly say nothing like that ever happened while we were filming the series – I didn't even know where I was going until the very last minute. No one told me a thing.

It was six o'clock in the evening by the time we arrived at the house. It was in a little town called Huthwaite, in the market square. The house was part of a terrace along one side of the square and on either side of it there were commercial buildings: an accountant's office and a betting shop which were empty at night when we would be filming. We were running slightly late, so I got straight down to business after taking only a minute to check myself in the mirror in the Winnebago and make sure that I looked presentable. There was no time for the luxury of a make up artist to make me feel like a film star.

I took a deep breath and walked through the front door of the house, which opened directly onto the pavement, with no front garden. As soon as I stepped inside I had a feeling of tremendous heaviness – the kind of pressure you get before a storm breaks. It was like the ceiling was pressing down on the room. My heart started pounding hard as if I was panicking. This was a family home; neat and tidy with comfortable chairs and magazines lying around. It wasn't decorated beautifully or anything like that but it was somewhere a family lived – a close family. Unfortunately, it didn't feel that way. The atmosphere was threatening. When I walked from the front room into the lounge next door it felt to me as if the house was sinking – as if it was hollow underneath.

The atmosphere continued to be very heavy in this second room and my heart was still racing. I put out my hand and touched the chimney breast that jutted out from the wall. The lounge was decorated in muted blues and greys.

'There have been noises heard from here,' I said, keeping my hand on the chimney. 'There has been growling – guttural noises and banging.'

The sensations confused me. It was so heavy and there had clearly been a lot going on. Already the house felt almost unbearably intense.

'I think this is the worst place I've ever been,' I said, and I hadn't even found the epicentre yet. That was my next job.

I was drawn back into the hallway and up the stairs, which is where I instinctively felt the centre of the haunting was located. I think that's why the ceiling downstairs felt as if it was pressing down. The haunting upstairs was so heavy that it was seeping down into the lower rooms – pressing and squeezing the house into the ground, which is why it felt as if it was sinking. As I mounted the stairs I still had the feeling that the house was unstable. It was like being on a ship – the place was rocking back and forth. I haven't ever felt that way before.

Upstairs and to the left there was an adult's bedroom simply decorated in pale cream with an orange and yellow border. At one side there was an iron bedstead with soft toys on the pillows. As I came through the doorway I started to shake and I felt disorientated. I put my hand against the wall to steady myself and realized that I felt sick. The atmosphere in the room was very uncomfortable and over in the corner, where there was a cloth wardrobe, I felt a strong presence of something dark. It turned out that there was a door into the attic behind the wardrobe, though we didn't film up there as it wasn't floored.

In any case, of more interest to me was the child's room on this floor. As I walked back across the hallway towards it I could feel that this was the epicentre of the problem.

'The energy in here just wants people out of the house,' I said.

The disoriented feeling that I had had on the stairs was even stronger in this room than anywhere else. It seemed so incongruous next to the boxes of children's toys by the bunk beds. The minute I crossed the doorway, even though the rest of the house felt heavy, the children's room was clearly different and the air pressure was dense, like a decompression chamber. The place felt so strange it was almost surreal and I was suspicious of it. What on earth had been going on here? It was as if the house wasn't part of the rest of the world – instead it was like stepping into a twilight zone. A place half here and half not. I thought that it was the doorway that I had sensed when I had done the psychometry. This room was only half in the material world; half of it was somewhere else.

'This is the strangest house I have ever been into,' I said.

Although I had opened myself to my instincts in the house and was working clairvoyantly I hadn't fully opened psychically, which would have called the spirit to me. As I came back down the stairs I was almost glad. This was going to be a difficult one to deal with. The atmosphere was so strong that I felt nervous about what I might be taking on, although at the same time it was intriguing. I had never felt anything like it.

Chris, the sceptic, was out in the garden as I left. He was talking about electromagnetic fields in haunted locations being the cause of paranormal experiences, rather than ghosts. As soon as I came outside I could feel the weight of the haunting lift from me. It was pretty well instant.

'Wow,' I thought, 'that was quick.'

Just to check I nipped back inside and immediately felt the pressure bear down on me again.

'Electromagnetic fields, eh?' I thought, walking back out of the door.

In the garden it was a sunny evening and I could feel my body relax. I stepped back into the doorway, one foot in, one foot out. 'That's a ghost. That's a strong presence,' I said. I could feel it on the left side of my body and not on the right. 'This one is going to be interesting.'

As Chris and Mark made their tour of the house I had time to recover fully. I really needed a chocolate bar and some coffee to get my energy back up. Claire, the production assistant I had met at the last house, got the kettle on and found some mint chocolate in the fridge, which restored me well. After I'd finished, Chris and Mark had done their rounds and it was time for me to go back into the house and meet the family.

When I got indoors I immediately liked Heather and her sisters, Tracey and Jane. They were well-built, healthy looking girls in their twenties and thirties with fresh faces, sitting on the sofa in the living room. Heather's two children had gone to stay with friends for the duration of the vigil and the clearing – something they had done a lot recently, due to the stress of living with this terrible presence. Straight away I had the impression they were a close family, although it was clear they were under a lot of strain because of what had been going on in the house. They were generous, warm women, not at all hysterical or the kind of people who would blow something up out of proportion. It was nice to see them bonded so closely as a family. I focused on Heather most of all because, after all, it was her house that was being haunted, so she was the reason I was there. She seemed nervous, her blue eyes darting backwards and forwards, but she put on a big smile and flicked her pony tail as I shook her hand. She had an eyebrow piercing that, I thought, made her seem a bit younger than she was. Although she was in her twenties she seemed to be only in her late teens. I could tell that she had a gift of her own – psychics are always aware of other psychics and Heather's aura was very silver and gold, which are the colours of someone with a strong spiritual life.

As if to prove the point, as we were sitting down, the spirit of a small boy, about ten or eleven years old, came into the room and stood close to Heather. I couldn't see him, only sense the essence of his spirit. He was not a trapped ghost, just a visitor. I think that probably happened around Heather a lot – very much as it happens around me. Spirits are attracted to those with psychic abilities because they want to communicate with them. In the past I have had spirits come to talk to me, to tell me something that is important to them. Once I saw a female visitor in a church and she showed me her gravestone as if to say 'Here, this is my name. This is where my body lies.' In general, ghosts don't have great truths to impart. They are sociable, though, and will tell you what is on their minds. I decided that Heather was quite nervous enough as it was and it was best not to tell her about the visiting child spirit. We had to focus on getting rid of the ghost who was causing the problem. That was the most urgent thing.

As I settled into my seat I suddenly had a vision of Heather, panicking, rushing out of the house in her pyjamas and running down the street.

'How odd,' I thought, but still, it was very vivid so I told her that is what I had seen.

'That's happened more than once,' Heather smiled. 'I'd sooner sleep on the bench outside than be sleeping in here.'

She had clearly been terrified by the haunting in her house, and as it turned out, she and her children had moved out a few weeks before and gone to stay with her sister because she couldn't bear the atmosphere in her own home. I couldn't blame her. The house was quite extraordinary and if you were sensitive in any way it would be difficult to live there.

The haunting had been tough on Heather. Her confidence had been badly knocked. Clairvoyantly, I could see that recently she had had a very difficult time with a relationship, leaving Heather with two young children to look after on her own. That kind of trauma had opened her up to the haunting because she was emotionally vulnerable and that, along with her psychic ability (which she had yet to tap into), meant that any ghost would be attracted to her.

'Don't worry,' I said. 'I won't leave here until it's over. It wouldn't be fair to leave you with a problem like this.'

Heather seemed to relax then, and I began to tell her about everything I had picked up as I went around the house on my own. She nodded as I told her about my sense of the noises, the bumps and the bangs. Apparently, these phenomena had been caught on film already.

September had given Heather a home camera and one night a few weeks before Heather and her sisters had set the cameras running and left the house, locking the door behind them. Three times in the couple of hours that the camera had been recording there were inexplicable knocks and noises from different places in the empty house.

'I feel also that this haunting has affected a child. That a child here has been visited,' I said.

Heather confirmed that the ghost had been terrifying her daughter, who was only five. The little girl, Carly Beth, said that her 'friends' came from a cupboard in the corner of her bedroom – the room I had identified as the epicentre of the haunting. She wanted 'them' to go away because she was scared. But Carly Beth had also been visited by the ghost of a girl called Chloe with whom she had made friends.

Chloe was harmless – a visiting spirit with no bad intentions – but one of Heather's main concerns was that the more sinister ghost who was causing the problems in the house might physically harm Carly Beth or her other daughter, Casey. Carly Beth had fallen down the stairs on two occasions after she had the sensation of being pushed on the upstairs landing. It is very rare for a ghost to physically hurt someone but the presence was so strong in the house I could quite believe that if any ghost was capable of it, then this was the one.

Heather had also experienced a vivid dream which, I think, might have been some kind of visionary experience. She said that in her dream she had woken to find a dark man sitting on her bed, threatening her. Then a priest appeared in the room and told her that she had to send the man away and to watch her children. She was scared that the priest meant that the children were in danger. This had really terrified her.

'I don't want to leave here,' Heather said. 'It's my house, whatever is going on. It's the spirit that ought to leave.'

'Do you think anyone has ever done something silly, like a ouija board?' I asked.

Heather shrugged her shoulders. 'Not while we've been here,' she said.

A ouija board did seem a likely explanation to me. With so much spirit activity in the property I reckoned something must have stirred it up to start with.

Tracey, the middle sister, then told me she had tracked down an old lady who used to live in Heather's house and was now in a nursing home nearby. The woman said that she had only managed to stay for six months and that Heather was doing well to have been there for over a year. She had also had the experience of a threatening male spirit coming to sit on the side of her bed.

'I couldn't stand it,' the old lady had said to Tracey.

This meant that the haunting clearly pre-dated Heather and her family moving into the house.

'Well it's going to be over now,' I promised. 'Will you stay tonight and do the vigil with me?'

It was easy to see that Heather didn't want to be in the house at night even if there were other people around her. But I do feel it is important to go through the vigil stage – to experience the haunting one last time in your home before it ends – because then you really feel and appreciate the difference once the ghost is gone. Heather looked nervous. After all, this was a woman who, on more than one occasion, had run away down the street in her nightwear.

'I'll be here with you,' I promised, and she bravely agreed that she would do it.

'It's my house,' she said again. 'It's the ghost that ought to be leaving.'

By this time it was getting late and we were all starving. I hadn't had anything proper to eat since the sandwich on the train and I knew we had a long night ahead of us. Claire said there was an Indian restaurant nearby and she organized a table for nine of us to eat there. Some of the crew had to stay behind in the house to set up camera equipment, although the ghost busting equipment was already in place. Mark had set up a thermal imaging camera, a sound recorder, electromagnetic sensors, movement sensors and thermometers, mostly in the children's bedroom as that was the epicentre of all the activity. The night vision cameras, however, still had to go in so we left the crew to it. Everyone else trooped out of the house for a curry. By the time we got to the restaurant I was really hungry, and the smell of the spices as we walked through the door made me feel like I was starving! My chicken korma was delicious and really hit the spot. Claire kindly organized a takeaway for the crew who had been left behind as we sat at the table and had some coffee and chocolates. Over the meal the girls told me more of their stories about the haunting. Heather's daughter Carly Beth was only five years of age. A few weeks before, she had tied a ribbon through the door handles of the cupboard in her room. She said that bad people were coming out of her closet and she didn't want it to open any more. It must have been awful for the kids living in that room, I thought. The feelings were so intense there that I couldn't imagine being able to sleep in that atmosphere.

As we gathered up our coats and Claire picked up the bags of hot naan breads and foil containers of curry, I walked into the street with Mark.

'Every one of Heather's stories sound plausible,' he said. 'This should be an interesting evening, Mia.'

I had to agree.

Claire went back to the house with the takeaway, but it was still quite early so the rest of us walked to a pub nearby called The White Dog. It was a lovely, old-fashioned English pub and we had a couple of drinks, biding our time until we were ready to start shooting.

Just before midnight I was back in the house with Mark and the three girls, Heather, Tracey and Jane. I had one last peek in the children's room with the lights on. The atmosphere still felt tense and heavy and I left the room after only a minute or two feeling very disorientated. It occurred to me that room was like a time warp – disconnected from the real world. By that stage I really felt it was a portal, a place where the barrier between this world and the spiritual world is very slight. This house was too open. As I walked back downstairs it was almost midnight – time for the lights to go out. We decided to start the vigil in the living room. Heather was so nervous I didn't want to subject her to the epicentre straight away and it seemed like a good place to kick things off.

'It'll be interesting to see what happens,' Chris said. 'I wonder if we will pick up anything on the equipment.'

'This house is badly haunted,' I told him. 'I think we're going to see some action tonight.'

He went back out into the Winnebago to watch us on the monitors and we settled down in the living room.

As midnight approached, the girls were quiet, shifting in their seats.

'Now remember, it can't hurt you,' I said. 'Don't panic and keep your torch beside you all the time.' Then the last of the camera crew signalled to me as he left the room and we were alone in the house.

'It's midnight. The lights are going off now. Three – two – one.'

And it was pitch black. It always takes a moment or two for my eyes to get accustomed but still it was difficult to see. Almost immediately I picked out orbs, sparkly lights, on the wall by the chimney breast. I didn't want to say anything to the girls because I didn't want to suggest anything to them. The lights were pretty, though, like fairly lights running up and down the wall. We sat in silence for a few minutes. Mark, it turned out, couldn't see the lights, but the girls described them later like glitter, though they wondered if it was only their eyes playing tricks on them.

After a while I took Mark upstairs to see what was going on up there. The chimney breast was directly underneath the child's room and I felt that the orbs were emanating from upstairs. The girls stayed downstairs, huddled together on the sofa. I could see how nervous the three of them were. It turned out that while Mark and I were away they all heard a banging, knocking noise in the kitchen beside them and had strange sensations of cold and headaches, and felt their faces and hair being stroked.

Meantime, Mark and I climbed the stairs, using our torches so as not to trip in the darkness. It was very, very black and my eyes couldn't seem to get used to it. The strange sensation I had had before, of the house rocking from side to side, continued as we climbed the stairs. When we went into the children's room it was as if we were bouncing off the walls. Mark began to laugh because it was so odd. We were stumbling, holding onto the furniture. I stood up against the wall to try to get my balance.

'This feels really weird,' Mark said. 'This room has a definite feeling, different from the rest of the house.'

It did. I was beginning to feel sick as if I was on a boat. The rocking was unpredictable, tilting in one direction and then another. After a few minutes we were both feeling unwell and decided to go back downstairs.

'It'll be nice to get out of here,' Mark said as we left the room.

Later, Mark did some measurements and brought a spirit level upstairs, but the house was pretty level – only a quarter of an inch out in one place, which couldn't possibly account for the odd feeling of random movement we had both experienced. It was strange. I had never felt anything like it.

Downstairs Heather, Tracey and Jane were feeling ill as well. We hadn't even been in the house for a full hour and everyone had experienced strange feelings and we were all at the stage of being quite unwell. I thought I might be sick from the movement of the upstairs bedroom. It was really disorientating. After only fifty minutes, at about ten to one we had had enough and everyone decided to go out to the Winnebago for a break.

'What do you think this is?' Mark asked me.

But I just didn't know what was going on. I had never experienced anything like it – Heather's home was like the Fun House at a carnival. Everything was distorted. It was weird, like stepping into some kind of distortion in reality.

'You've certainly got a strange house,' I told her.

After a cup of tea and a chat in the Winnebago I asked Heather if she would go back inside with me. She wasn't keen, but I felt it was important for her to come. It was her house, after all. She said that she had never experienced the strange rocking feeling both Mark and I had felt upstairs, and I wanted to see if she might feel it too if she came with me.

'By doing this tonight,' I promised her, 'you'll feel the difference tomorrow when I clear the house.'

Upstairs Heather laughed when she felt the motion in Carly Beth and Casey's room.

'I've never had that before,' she said.

But it was exactly the same thing that Mark and I had experienced earlier.

We went to her bedroom as well as the children's room. I held her hand the whole time as we propped ourselves up against the wall for support and at one point she went rigid with fear. It was making both of us feel sick. I didn't like doing this to Heather and we quickly decided to go back outside. It was worrying me that I didn't know what on earth was going on. No one seemed to have any explanations for the rocking sensation, which was unusual. Usually Mark had read or heard of something similar whenever we came up against something new, but this time he was stumped. Chris couldn't come up with anything either and even he said that he had a strange feeling in the children's room that left him unsettled, although he didn't feel the full force of the tilting that the rest of us had.

'It must be bad if Chris can feel it,' I joked.

'It's probably autosuggestion from you lot,' he retorted, a sceptic until the end.

By four in the morning everyone was exhausted and we went to the hotel where Gemma had arranged for my bag to be delivered to my room. I didn't even unpack. I sat up for a long time by the window, smoking cigarettes and trying to figure it out. I probably should have asked Eric, but I wanted to think things through for myself. The bedroom was certainly some kind of portal, I decided. A place where the fabric between this world and the next was thin, and reality was twisted out of shape. Heather's emotional crisis with her boyfriend and her psychic sense had made her vulnerable and she acted like a magnet for psychic activity, but the place itself was odd – as if it had been opened up. It felt *too* open.

'I'll have to be careful,' I thought.

After the sun came up I finally fell into bed.

No one else got much sleep that night, either. The crew said they felt disorientated and strange. When I woke up, around ten, the sky was covered in dark clouds and it was pouring with rain. I decided to go for a walk, but it became torrential and when I got back to the hotel, drenched through, people were assembling downstairs, ordering food. I grabbed something to eat quickly, and then went back up to my room and lay on top of the bed – after changing into some warm, dry clothes.

'I'm fine, aren't I Eric?' I said.

'Yes,' Eric replied. 'You're going to be fine. Don't worry.'

But I couldn't get it out of my mind that there was a portal in that bedroom and I wasn't sure what that really meant. I didn't know if getting rid of the spirit who was scaring the family would close it. I hoped so.

I could feel Eric's presence beside me. He felt very reassuring which, I decided, meant that if I cleared the spirit, the house would be fine.

'It'll be fine,' I repeated. 'I've got you there to help me, Eric, and keep me safe.'

That evening everyone went to the local pub for dinner while the crew rigged the cameras in the house for the clearing. I picked at a chicken and mushroom pie as I thought about what might be waiting for us at the house. The girls were up at the bar, chatting animatedly to the bar staff, who they clearly knew. It was nice to see them in conversation – being normal.

'Are you nervous?' Claire asked me.

I nodded. 'You've found me a real doozy here,' I said.

Around midnight we went back to the house. The crew had set things up in the downstairs room, right under the children's bedroom, which was too small for everyone to fit in so had been discounted as the location for the clearing.

'Try to stay calm,' I told the girls as we sat down at the table which was decked out with a sea of candles.

'It looks really pretty in here,' Heather said nervously.

'Now, it's time to get down to business,' I started. 'Once I have started I won't stop. You might feel sensations but this ghost can't harm you physically and anything that happens will pass.'

I checked that everyone was ready and then closed my eyes and took a deep breath. It was time for me to open up psychically. I started to search the house, outside my body, looking for the spirit. There was no one on the stairs. I went up into Heather's bedroom and again there was no one there. So I crossed the hall into the children's room and there was a figure just standing in front of the closed cupboard. It was a man in his late fifties and I had the sense that he was from the 1890s. He was balding and wore a browny-beige, rough shirt and a leather waistcoat with no pockets and dark trousers that seemed to be made of some coarse material. He had a mark around his neck as if he had been hanged or strangled. When he spoke he had an indistinct voice and it was difficult to hear what he was saying, but he told me that his name was Jack Pullman. At least his surname sound like Pullsomething. After that he didn't speak any more and the information he wanted to communicate to me came in the form of pictures.

Jack wasn't keen to come downstairs, but I backed out of the room slowly and motioned for him to follow. Gently, I brought him down and into the room where the clearing had been set up. He was standing beside the table right where Tracey was sitting as I returned to my body. In my mind's eye I began to see pictures from his life. There was an image of cattle being herded into a tight place in daylight. And then cattle in droves in the market square outside the house. I saw butchers' hooks lined up at a slaughterhouse. He had been hanged, I saw, and had gone to the pub first. This confused me at the time, but later the girls told me that the local pub had indeed been the location of many hangings. More than anything, though, I had a sense of intense rage. Jack was furious. He had been hung for a crime – something to do with cattle, I was sure – but he hadn't committed this crime alone and was angry that he had died without his accomplice. Jack believed strongly that this man should have died with him, so he had stayed behind, revelling in his rage, to search for the accomplice who he felt had cheated him.

'Why have you been terrorizing women and children in this house?' I asked him.

Jack seemed unaware of this. I think he was so caught up in his anger that he really didn't see or consider anyone or anything else. He couldn't care less. We've all had that in our lives, I suppose. Feeling so angry, or confused or frustrated that we lose a sense of anything going on around us. Jack was totally taken up with his fury.

'And the room rocking upstairs?' I asked him, pushing for some kind of explanation.

Then I had the sense that the feeling generated upstairs had been Jack trying to scare me. He knew that strange noises, cold patches, headaches and the feeling of being touched wouldn't trouble me at all. So he had distorted reality. He was an angry person, so infused with ill-will that he was just out for a spot of badness wherever he could find it. It struck me as sad that he had stayed behind in this angry, almost tortured state, looking for an accomplice who had long since died.

I have experienced that feeling of sadness before. Once I sent over the spirit of a young Victorian girl who had been raped and murdered near a fairground by the man she had invited to accompany her there. When she died she had been dismissed as a 'loose woman' – someone who wasn't morally upright because (people believed) she was available for sex before marriage. They said that she had got what she deserved. The girl was so upset she couldn't go over to the other side when she died and had stayed to try to clear her name. Even though sex before marriage had long since ceased to be that kind of moral issue for most people, this poor girl was still upset, still wandering, confused, trying to get over her discomfort and recover from the slur on her character long after it had any relevance. Those strong feelings take up too much energy. It is tragic.

Now here I was with Jack, who had spent years terrorizing people in this house because he couldn't let go of his anger and simply move on. I decided it was time to send him over. He had caused enough chaos and I didn't think I would find out anything else of interest.

'I am sending Jack over,' I said.

Then Eric appeared beside me and a doorway of light opened by the chimney breast. I began to say the De Profundis prayer and Eric placed his hand lightly on Jack's arm. Jack seemed to relax, and put up no resistance to Eric as he guided him away. I watched happily, and with great relief, as they walked together through the doorway. As the portal closed I could feel the atmosphere in the room lift. Around the chimney breast there were showers of golden, glittery lights. I had never seen that before anywhere. It was as if the whole house was being cleansed by it. I smiled because it was so beautiful. Golden snow.

The girls could feel the difference too. In fact, all three of them were very sensitive – Tracey had felt a cold sensation next to her when Jack had come into the room and stopped at her end of the table. The four of us walked around the house together to check it over. The rooms upstairs felt normal again and I opened the cupboard door in Carly Beth and Casey's bedroom and was delighted to see that all there was in there was clothes. The transformation had been dramatic and miraculous.

'You've changed my life,' Heather breathed, her blue eyes sparkling as she gave me a hug, while Tracey and Jane went to fetch some flowers from the kitchen that they had bought to give me.

I felt elated. It was great to see the place so much better than it was before. As the crew packed up I wasn't sure that the whole thing hadn't been started by someone messing around with a ouija board, but we would have no way to prove that as it had probably happened a long time ago. I just felt that the place had been in such chaos and the feelings so heavy that something must have kick-started the experience and let Jack in. It didn't matter now though. The place felt light and happy and Heather felt better already.

'You need to look after yourself and get your confidence back,' I told her. 'You have a gift too, you know. You just have to open it.' Heather just smiled shyly and said thanks again.

'I'll never forget this house,' I said to Mark as we were in the car going back to the hotel. 'I'm learning new things all the time. I've been psychic for over twenty years and this series is like being on a fast track – so many big instances all at once.'

Mark nodded. 'Are you excited?' he said.

'Yes,' I admitted. 'I suppose I am. I wonder what we are in for next week?' I didn't even know where we were going. Mark shrugged his shoulders – he was as much in the dark as I was.

'Well. We'll just have to see,' I said and settled down, leaning my head against the top of the seat. Now it was over I felt exhausted. I caught sight of myself in the rear view mirror. 'God,' I thought, 'I look knackered.' My aura was completely flat with flecks of pink around the edges because I had been so stressed out at the house.

'I'd better get some sleep tonight,' I said.

And I did. I slept like a baby.

Chapter Four

The Elvin Family's House. Newcastle.
Cleared on 4th September 2005.

The Elvins have been living in their house for three and a half years and have experienced paranormal phenomena during all of that time. These phenomena include inexplicable noises, the angry voice of a man, orbs and a feeling of acute discomfort upstairs in the house, particularly in the boys' bedroom. Three members of the family (including two of the children) have seen the sinister figure of a man with no facial features. Members of the family have also been touched and pulled. A medium has come to the house in the past but has not succeeded in stopping the activity.

Life Is Pleasant. Death Is Peaceful.
It's the Transition that Can Be Troublesome.

By the time I received my next train ticket to Newcastle I was excited. I had realized what a tremendous opportunity this series was and how I now had the chance to develop my skills by using them in this very concentrated way. It was like having a couple of years' worth of experiences all at once and though that would stretch me, I was looking forward to it. The cameras didn't make me so nervous any more and I was finding my stride.

Mostly I don't get scared when dealing with ghosts. Saying that is almost a challenge to the spirit world, I know, and I am nervous about writing it because it's tempting fate. But it really is very rare that I am jumpy or terrified for a moment. Much more likely is the fascination I always feel; the draw of paranormal activity. Ghosts are so individual. Although all have been through the same experience of death, they have different reasons for choosing to stay behind, and find different ways to express themselves and to relate to the material world. While the trapped spirits I was going to be dealing with in every one of these houses were clearly all extreme cases and had extreme emotions around them, each one had his or her own way of communicating. Jack, the spirit at Heather's house, had found a way of doing so that was new to me: to distort reality so that the house seemed to be moving. What might the next spirits come up with? It intrigued me.

And of course, the main thing was that I felt I could really help. I get tremendous satisfaction from clearing a house of a disruptive spirit and letting a family get back to normal. It's the best part of what I do – seeing families together and happy after the difficult experience of a haunting.

I took the train to Newcastle – my next destination – and then changed for Cramlington, where Claire and Gemma picked me up. This time we went to the hotel first – a Premier Lodge nearby where I was booked into my usual smoking room. I dumped my bag, only half unpacking it – I flung my nightie on the bed and my toothbrush in the bathroom and checked the view from the window. Then it was time to go and do the psychometry.

When we arrived at the second hotel, the place was all set up and there was no waiting around. The girls had used the same tablecloth and props as on previous occasions. It was only the objects themselves that were different. I didn't have a great deal of feeling about a lot of the items laid out before me. In fact, I had a bit of a giggle – they didn't seem personal or precious enough to pick up much psychometric activity. Objects have to be around a lot of paranormal activity or else be very treasured possessions for me to be able to get much in the way of useful information from them. I surveyed the bits and pieces laid out on the cloth and had doubts – they just didn't seem important enough, somehow.

'Well, I'll give it a try,' I said.

I picked up a luminous green, plastic ball, the kind that kids play with, and I didn't feel anything at all.

'No dice with that,' I explained, setting it aside.

Next there was a fine gold chain, a silver ring and a hoop earring with a gold twist. I tried these next but didn't pick up anything paranormal; only that the wearer of the earring was female and had a tummy problem, that the chain had felt tight around the wearer's neck and that the silver ring belonged to a man who knew about the paranormal but was sceptical. Then there was a child's blanket that also gave me no unusual feelings; only those of comfort and cosiness.

'This isn't going too well, is it?' I joked, picking up the next object, which was another child's toy – this time a green crocodile. From this I did get the feeling that it had moved inappropriately and that there had been a good deal of fear around it.

'This toy does things it shouldn't do,' I said. 'I think it has moved on its own.'

Last of all, I turned my attention to a bookend and a silver candlestick. These, I felt, belonged in the same place together in a lounge. I could sense strong feelings around them. From both I had a sensation of smoke. I could smell it, the sensation was so strong. This wasn't the house burning, it was something else. And with the smoke came fear. I felt uncomfortable touching both of these objects and picked up the same feeling of heaviness that I often sense in haunted locations – that feeling of heavy air pressure like the atmosphere before a storm. Although I hadn't picked up a wide spread of information, I knew that certainly there had been some kind of paranormal activity in this place.

'Ah, right,' I said. 'There's something live in this house. We've got a haunting.'

As usual no one gave anything away to me. The crew dismantled the room and Gemma said that she would drop me back at the hotel – the crew had to go and do some filming at the house before any experts were allowed in to see it. They wanted to get the interviews with the family in the can. Claire told me that I wouldn't be needed again until the next day. It was late in the afternoon and I was left on my own. Back at the hotel I realized I was hungry so I went to the restaurant in the pub next door and ordered some salmon mornay and vegetables and a vodka and orange, and settled down in a comfortable booth on my own. What a rare treat these days!

'I could have a bubble bath,' I thought, 'and watch some TV.'

I certainly felt that I wanted to measure my energies and I wondered what the sense of acrid smoke I had picked up from the objects was all about. It struck me that perhaps it was only that they were usually situated on a mantelpiece or somewhere that might be very smoky. It seemed pretty unlikely, though, and my instinct was that smoke and fire would be very important in this haunting.

After dinner I went back to the hotel, headed for my room, ran a bath and sat in the hot tub smoking and reading a magazine for a while. It was nice to have a night off. I made myself a cup of tea and curled up in front of the television.

'Bliss,' I thought. 'I bet I'm not relaxed like this, this time tomorrow!'

The next morning when I awoke I was disturbed by an odd dream I had had during the night. It had the vivid feel of a premonition where you know that you aren't asleep, although what's happening is very surreal. I had the clear image of a woman with long, dark hair and high cheekbones. There was a two-storey house that was painted white. And I could see the name John. At this time no one had told me anything about the family or where they lived and my first assumption was that this dream perhaps had something to do with the hotel we were staying in and that I was picking up on spirit energy from my room. I always book newly built hotels, if I am choosing for myself, as it reduces the chances of paranormal activity which will disturb my sleep. Sometimes it is difficult to switch off. In fact, even when I am switched off, some ghosts will still come and look for attention.

Anyway, I got dressed and wandered downstairs where I met Linda, one of the production team. We ordered eggs, toast and tea and as we were eating I told her about my dream. Linda's eyes flashed and she ran her hand through her short, red hair.

'Wow,' she said. 'That's the family you're going to today. That's the name of the husband. And his wife is a brunette – she has long hair. She has high cheekbones too. Amazing.'

That interested me, the fact that I had a premonition like that. I thought it must mean that the family really needed me because I was so much drawn to them psychically before actually meeting them.

I went back up to my room and Linda arranged for a new hair and make-up guy, Michael, to come and make sure that I looked OK. Michael was nice. He was in his thirties, married with a son, and he buzzed around the room applying my lipstick and blow-drying my hair while we chatted about this and that. It was becoming quite a trial having my hair and make up done so often – I was bored with spending so much time looking at myself in the mirror. I just couldn't wait to get into the house.

When I was ready, Gemma knocked on the door and said she had come to drive me to the house. I checked myself in the mirror. Michael had done a good job and I thanked him. Then Gemma and I wandered out to the car park and got going.

There was no direct approach to where the Elvins lived because the house was part of a terrace which was located in a close. There was a sloping alleyway from the road with wide steps and I walked from where Gemma had parked. It was a normal estate. There were window boxes and potted plants outside some of the front doors. I could hear laughter and dogs barking and all the normal noises you get wherever people live. It certainly wasn't the kind of place most people would think there would ever be a ghost problem – no dungeons, no ancient monuments, no creaky old doors. Instead, there were half a dozen kids playing on the steps, throwing a ball around.

One of them came up when he noticed me, a boy who looked about thirteen.

'Are you that psychic?' he said.

I had been on *This Morning* the week before and had noticed people looking at me more than usual, even just in shops or on the street.

'Do you get rid of ghosts? Is it scary?' the boy insisted.

I never want to frighten anyone, least of all kids.

'No, darling, it's like making a phone call and the angels come to get them,' I told him reassuringly. I hope he wasn't too disappointed!

Then I got to the Elvins' house. There were flowers outside and a pebble fountain with a few gnomes around it. I stood at the door for a second and didn't feel anything at all coming from the property.

'God, I hope the crew haven't wasted their time,' I thought. 'That would be a disaster.'

I needn't have worried. The minute I walked inside the front door I felt that familiar, heavy, oppressive feeling; that typical pre-storm sensation affecting the air pressure. The house itself was light and bright. It was very clean with a sparkling laminate floor and bright paintings on the walls. But the feeling in there was dreadful, as if there was electrical friction buzzing around in the atmosphere. I picked up a sensation of acute distress, even panic in the hallway. This wasn't a happy home. There was something paranormal in this house and it was causing a lot of problems and a lot of fear.

I moved from the hallway into the clean, light kitchen, where I sensed that although it wasn't the centre of the activity there had been light anomalies seen and scraping sounds heard. Electrical items had been switched on and off and there was a strong sense of fear in the room. I stood beside the cream-coloured kitchen table and took in the atmosphere for a moment.

'Weird stuff has happened in here,' I said.

It struck me again how normal the room looked. It was light and spotless and even smelt faintly of toast. But there was definitely something very wrong there. I could feel it.

Then I moved on to the living room. There again, I had a strong sense that people had seen and heard things in the room, although it still wasn't the centre of what had been going on. The action was really elsewhere and had only spilled over into these downstairs rooms.

Back out in the hallway I felt drawn upstairs. This interested me – the last houses had all had the epicentres of their hauntings on the upper floors. This isn't always the case, but there seemed to be a pattern emerging. As I climbed the stairs I noticed a wind chime hanging up and I thought that this was responsible for one of the noises which had been heard. I suddenly knew that this wind chime had sounded when there was no wind at all and the noise had scared people. My chest became tight and heavy as I got up to the landing and my heart rate began to rise. I knew I was getting closer to the centre of it.

Upstairs there were three bedrooms. One was a beautifully decorated pink and white room which clearly belonged to a little girl. A lot of love and care had gone into putting this room together – there were castles painted on the wall and a gorgeous toy canopy bed with lots of dolls on it. The feeling in there was heavy, though, and although, again, it wasn't the epicentre, I didn't want to stay in there any longer than I had to. My instinct was to stay out of the room, as if there was a force in there that wanted me gone.

The next room I went into was decorated in lilac and white, and belonged to the adults in the house. Again it was beautifully decorated with a pretty, sheer canopy over the bed. I had a strong feeling that someone had been pushed or pulled out of the bed there. This room had been the scene of tremendous sadness, and many sleepless nights had been spent in there because of the haunting. As I passed into the room, my chest tightened in the area just at the doorway. I felt a very heavy feeling in that area and I thought that strong spirit activity had gone on there, perhaps even an apparition that had caused extreme panic for the people who lived in the house.

Last of all there was a boy's bedroom decorated in blue with steel bunk beds and lots of boys' toys. Again, care had been taken in the decoration of this room and the place was spotless, but out of everywhere in the house it was in this room that the feeling was at its worst. It is unusual for kids' rooms to feel so heavy and it made me angry that children had again been frightened. Nice people don't scare kids, neither do nice ghosts. This was another malevolent spirit who liked to cause trouble. Over in the corner, beside the cupboard, the atmosphere was so dense that it was like walking into hot soup.

'God, what an awful feeling. This is the epicentre,' I said. 'It's not a good sign either that it is in a child's room. I need to meet the family before I can go any further.'

As I came downstairs the other experts, Mark and Chris, had just arrived to do their walk through. I went to stand outside and have a cigarette while I gathered my thoughts. Everything that had happened in this house was designed to scare people, particularly kids. From the walk through I knew there had been apparitions that had terrorized the family.

'It's taking pleasure in frightening people,' I thought. 'But I don't scare easily. It isn't going to worry me.'

It came into my mind that the haunting here might well be down to poltergeist activity. Poltergeist activity is mischievous in the extreme – designed to scare and to attract attention. Sometimes this is triggered by humans, rather than ghosts; most normally teenagers who have psychic abilities but haven't yet learned to control them. Other times a ghost is out to get attention, to cause fear and feed off that energy. In neither case is it a good sign, and this house had the hallmarks of poltergeist goings-on all over it. It wasn't just light orbs, or some crashing, there had definitely been terrifying full-scale apparitions here. I finished my cigarette and Claire came out and said it was time for me to meet the Elvins.

Inside, Katrina was exactly as I had seen her in my dream the night before – a pretty, warm brunette with lovely high cheekbones. John, her husband, sat beside her, clearly uncomfortable with the whole process of having cameras and all these strangers in his house. He was a slender guy with blue eyes and a shaved head. It was clear to me straight away that Katrina was more sensitive to the spirit in the house. She was the one who had the sleepless nights.

'You don't believe her,' I said to John.

'I tend to think it could be down to something else,' he admitted.

This seemed strange to me. There was something about John that I picked up. He had some spiritual background in his family, I felt, but he was blocking out those feelings. Later he told me that his mother was a medium, but that up until now he hadn't believed in ghosts.

The Elvins were a close and happy couple and I didn't sense any clear, emotional cause that had made them vulnerable to the haunting. This also was slightly unusual as in most houses there is a trigger event in the life of someone in the family that makes them more sensitive to the spirit world. It always strikes me as unfair, that just when you're down you are given the extra burden of paranormal activity around you, but sadly that's often the way that it happens. Extreme loss, sadness or stress make people more susceptible to an awareness of the paranormal.

I told the Elvins what I had felt as I walked around their house and Katrina confirmed there had been apparitions in the doorway of her bedroom and that one of her sons had seen the same apparition that she had. He called it a 'monster man': the solid, dark figure of a man with no face.

'It's deliberately trying to scare you. Everything that has happened is frightening,' I said. 'You have a hive of poltergeist activity here. It's good for us, but I'm afraid it's scary for you. Don't worry, though. I will be here tonight to do the vigil. You won't spend one more night in this house on your own until it's gone.'

When I said this Katrina covered her eyes and started crying. John put his hand out to comfort her.

'Are you OK?' I asked.

She had clearly been under tremendous strain and it took her a few minutes before she could speak again.

'And do you think it's one spirit or more than one?' she asked.

My sense was that it was only one ghost. After all, that's rare enough, never mind there being a multiple haunting, but the truth was that I didn't know yet. Until I was able to open fully at the clearing I wouldn't have the details. I was only working clairvoyantly up until that point.

I felt sorry for the Elvins. Later that afternoon I met their kids, briefly. They were going over to their uncle's place to stay while we dealt with the haunting in the house. There were two boys and a little girl – clearly a close and loving family.

'Don't worry. We'll sort this. I promise,' I said to Katrina after the kids had gone. We had some pizza in the Winnebago while the crew set up the camera equipment and Mark placed his sensors around the house.

I was sure that we were going to see some amazing phenomena that evening. The ghost was clearly looking for attention and here we were, an eager audience.

'You're all just suggestible,' Chris the sceptic teased.

It surprised me that Chris didn't sense anything. Nothing at all. He was really interested in what was going on, but hadn't picked up anything out of the ordinary on his walk through this house or any of the others. It's unusual for someone to be so interested and yet so closed. But this was a poltergeist and I hoped that perhaps this spirit would break the mould.

Katrina and John had been given a camera by September a few weeks before and when they went through the footage they had discovered that a sound recording had been taken in their sons' bedroom in the middle of the night. It was a man's voice, very indistinct but definitely there, and it had a tone of surprising animosity. Katrina thought that it said, 'Don't touch me.'

Mark loaded the recording onto his ghost-busting computer and analysed it. It was clearly speech, he said, and the voice of someone not in the house at the time. He reckoned it said, 'Don't try and talk,' or perhaps, 'John, don't speak,' when he looked at the sound waves. I don't understand any of that technical stuff but it really fascinated me, nonetheless. There was no easy explanation for the voice on the recording although there was an outside chance that it had been cast up from the street, perhaps, or from the house next door. Wherever it came from I was looking forward to getting into the house and getting the lights off to see and hear for myself!

At last, close to midnight, everything was ready. We decided to start in the kitchen, where there had been a lot of activity, even though it wasn't the epicentre of the problem. The crew left Mark, Katrina, John and I in there while Chris monitored us from the Winnebago. At midnight I gave my now usual talk about using torches and remembering that nothing can really hurt you, then it was three – two – one and the lights went out.

As my eyes adjusted I settled down in my seat to wait. Katrina and I were at one end of the table together and only a few minutes into the vigil we both looked over in John's direction at the same time to see a huge amount of light activity around his head. It was almost as if he was lit up. Katrina's hands shot up over her mouth. 'That is the strangest thing I've ever seen in my life,' she said.

The lights were strong and definite and were flickering around John's head and shoulders and flying upwards through the ceiling. John couldn't see a thing, but sat stock still while we marvelled at the light show around him. It was almost as if the ghost was pointing at him, lighting him up.

After a while the lights subsided, trailing off through the ceiling, and the room became dark again. Katrina and I were both freezing cold – in fact, Mark felt our hands because he thought it was a trick. It was a warm night and the infra-red cameras acted like heaters, so it should have been quite hot in the room, but he confirmed that our hands were icy.

'I'd be quite interested if Mark and I went upstairs,' I said, thinking that we could follow the orb lights upwards and see if they led to anything else that might be going on up there.

John and Katrina agreed to stay in the kitchen while Mark and I climbed the stairs carefully, our torches pointed downwards so we wouldn't trip. We decided to bide our time in the hallway for a while to see which rooms we might feel drawn to. I kept seeing shadows out of the corner of my eye which left me feeling frustrated because I wanted to see properly. It was tempting to open up my psychic sense fully, but I was strict with myself and stuck to what I could feel in my normal senses and clairvoyantly. Mark and I decided to sit down on the floor, putting our backs against opposite walls. We had been there only a minute or two when we heard a strange banging noise on the steps.

'That's a bloody weird noise,' I commented, as we peered down. There was no one there.

We waited a few more minutes and my mind began to wander. Sitting around for ages in the dark, it can be difficult to concentrate and you can't stay too focused. As soon as my mind was completely relaxed I saw a dark, dark shadow about a foot away from me on my right. Out of this a man's shape materialized. It was around five feet nine inches in height and of stocky build, and it came together in the doorway of John and Katrina's room. It was too dark for me to be able to make out any features on his face but I could see the figure very clearly, as clearly as if it was Mark standing next to me. None of this showed up on the camera, but the apparition made me flinch as it appeared out of nowhere and moved suddenly towards me. Mark was in one of the bedrooms at this stage and said that right after I had seen it in the hallway he had seen the same apparition in the bedroom and, also, a reflection of it in one of the mirrors. What he saw was shimmering, as if the apparition was materializing slowly.

'It was in the mirror on the right. I'm sure I saw its reflection,' he said.

We both felt it was amazing and we were excited. Although Mark has a lot of experience in haunted locations, more than half the time he didn't see anything particularly definite while he was conducting his investigations. It's the same for me – most hauntings are far gentler than the kind experienced by the families on *Haunted Homes*. For us, this was a real treat. In house after house we were experiencing the same phenomena together. That is quite important to me – that we were seeing and feeling the same things. It doesn't usually work like that – often I am the only person to really tune in to the spirit. It was nice to be able to share that experience with someone else.

It was time to go into the epicentre of this haunting. In the boys' bedroom the feeling was heavy and unpleasant. It made both Mark and I want to run away. We stood face to face so that we could clearly see both sides of the room and waited. Almost straight away we both saw the same man again. The figure appeared in the corner of the room, so strongly that we both jumped. Again it was very dark so neither of us could see detail (I could hardly see Mark's face at all, never mind the features of the shady character in the corner). It disappeared immediately and we both went over and stood where it had been.

'It's either tagging on to us or we've been very lucky,' I said.

But both Mark and I felt that this ghost wanted to be seen. He had been hoping to scare us and, in fact, he had. We had both jumped more than once because he had appeared and disappeared so suddenly.

'That's poltergeists for you,' I said.

I wanted to bring Katrina up into the boys' bedroom now. I wanted her to really experience the haunting in her house for the last time. I thought this would give her a solid sense of closure when I came to clear the place the next day, so I felt it was important for her to have as many experiences tonight as possible.

Mark took John out to the Winnebago where they would be able to monitor our progress. I asked Katrina to come upstairs to her sons' bedroom with me, to see if she might experience what Mark and I had seen earlier.

'I avoid this room like the plague,' she said as we came through the doorway.

'Here, hold my hand if you like,' I offered.

I could sense how nervous she was.

'This is the last time, isn't it?' she said.

'Yes, it's your last time. I promise.'

Again the activity that came was in the corner of the room beside the boys' cupboard. This time there wasn't a full-scale apparition. However, the corner pulsed much darker than the rest of the room all of a sudden, as if the ghost was trying to come together into a spectre, but didn't quite manage to do so. Katrina moved behind me and said she didn't want to look. She was petrified.

In the Winnebago, John was apparently convinced that this was a shadow from the cupboard itself, but neither Katrina nor I felt that was what we had seen. It was sudden. It came and went. There was no normal explanation for it.

'I think you've been really brave. Well done on coming upstairs,' I told Katrina.

It was a really eventful evening, but Chris was still sceptical. We went for a cup of tea outside while he decided to go around the house in the dark on his own. I noticed, though, that as he did so, he kept the torch on the whole time! Then he pronounced that he'd be perfectly willing to sleep in the boys' room exactly where we'd seen the apparition.

'He's just exhausted. He's dying to get to bed!' I joked.

Chris, as ever, was markedly more relaxed than anyone else at the location all night. He simply didn't pick up anything at all.

It was almost time for dawn to break. John, Katrina and I went back into the kitchen.

'It's been an amazing night,' I said. 'And I know what I have seen here. I know there is a ghost in your house. And I know you know that too, Katrina. I promise that I will clear this house tomorrow night. For you, John, even though you're not sure what to think, the nicest thing is that after tomorrow your wife won't be scared any more, and neither will your children. I really want to sort this out for you.'

It was light by the time I got back to the hotel room and collapsed onto the bed.

'Wow,' I said to myself. Even for me that was an amazing experience. Ghosts usually don't try to scare me. Most ghosts wouldn't dream of trying to scare anyone. But again, here was one that had made me jump. I often have the physical symptoms of fear – a raised heart rate, a heightened sensitivity – but those symptoms are normally only physical and a reaction to the presence of the paranormal. I don't actually start or flinch when I see a spirit or when one moves towards me.

'Heavy,' I murmured and I fell asleep.

When I woke up it was after lunchtime. I stumbled into the bathroom blearily and saw from my reflection that I hadn't managed to make it into my nightie the night before. I ran a bath and poured in some nice, smelly bubbles and then I switched on the radio. I had slept really well and felt refreshed. There was a muffin on the dressing table beside the kettle, so I ate it with a cup of tea and reckoned that would be enough for breakfast. Then I slipped into the bath and luxuriated for a while.

It was late in the afternoon by the time I made it downstairs into the hotel lobby. Most of the crew had surfaced and there was a plan for everyone to have a meal at a local carvery before we went to do the clearing. I hadn't eaten anything apart from the muffin since the night before and my appetite was really kicking in. I was starving. We set off in the car. Gemma had called ahead and booked a huge table for about fourteen of us and we all tucked into a hearty roast dinner. As I was eating it flickered through my mind that I had in fact promised the Elvins that I would remove their ghost. I had a sudden anxiety attack that I shouldn't be so confident. It was all down to me, really, so what would happen if I couldn't find the ghost in their house this evening, or if Eric for some reason couldn't take him over? There was no way to rehearse; no way to check. I had never found myself unable to help before, but still, I had gone on camera and said I could do it. I had promised the family I could do it. What if I couldn't?

I slipped quietly away from the table and stood outside, smoking a cigarette, feeling my stomach churning. I knew I had to do my best – no one could ask for anything more – but this was a tricky ghost. This ghost had actually scared me. I didn't want to let anybody down and not knowing how it was going to go was suddenly unnerving.

'Oh, get on with it girl,' I chided myself, taking one last draw on my cigarette.

'You're going to be there, aren't you, Eric?'

'Always,' came back the reply.

'Right.'

We got to the house quite late and the crew got on with rigging up the cameras. We had decided to do the clearing in the kitchen because it would be easy to position everyone around the table there. Claire and Gemma set up an array of candles all over the room and the crew bustled around checking light and sound levels while I chatted to John and Katrina. My stomach was still churning and my adrenalin was up.

'I can't believe this one actually scared me. On camera. I'm going to be scared on TV,' I said to Katrina. 'Mia Dolan, expert psychic.'

She smiled reassuringly. 'Me too,' she said, and I had to take her point.

It was midnight by the time we got going. I sat at the end of the table with Katrina next to me and John next to her. The room looked lovely with the light from the candles setting off the cream-coloured walls. It just glowed. I explained that I was going to psychically search the house for the ghost, bring him back to the kitchen and ask him some questions to see if there was any explanation for what had been going on. Then Eric would come and help him over. Once again, I made it clear that once I had started I wouldn't stop. I knew this always made the crew nervous because there could be no second take, but once I am into a clearing and have become fully open psychically I have to keep going. I have to give it my complete attention, my best shot, every time.

The room fell silent and I closed my eyes, reaching out with my spirit, into the hallway and up the stairs. I expected to meet the ghost in the boys' bedroom which, after all, was the epicentre of the haunting, but he was waiting for me at the top of the stairs, outside the cupboard in the hallway. It was a man, the same size and build as the apparition I had seen the night before. This time, though, I could see the detail of his face and body. His clothes were ragged and his face completely scarred. It looked as if he had been burned and suddenly all the premonitions I had had about smoke made complete sense. The ghost glared at me as if daring me to be upset by his appearance. It was horrible and I knew this man had suffered an agonizing death. He was carrying some kind of chain with a tag on the end. I motioned to him to follow me and slowly backed down the stairs, leading him into the kitchen, where he stood at the end of the table beside John.

I could smell an awful stench in the room then – the smell of rotting meat. The ghost told me that his name was Jack and that he had been burned to death in a place where he couldn't see because it was so dark. He had also been unable to breathe. Jack had clearly been trapped in a fire. He told me that this was his area, and that there had been a colliery here, which was where he had died. Then he pointed to John.

'He knows,' he said.

I realized that John was the reason this spirit had come to the house. John was the connection. I had known there had to be some reason for the haunting coming to the Elvins rather than any other family, and this time it hadn't been an emotional trauma that simply left someone open to it. This time the ghost had chosen John for a reason: John's grandfather.

'Did your grandfather work in a colliery here?'

'Yes,' John confirmed. 'As a boy.'

'That's the connection,' I said. 'Your grandfather was at the colliery when this accident happened. He was there at the time this man died.'

I saw that the ghost hadn't only been a worker in the colliery. Either he owned it or he ran it, but he was certainly in charge. He told me that a lot of people had died with him. He was furious. First, because he felt he should have had more of a life, but there was also something else.

'Tell them I didn't do it,' he said, banging his hands down on the table.

I realized that he had somehow been blamed for the accident at the mine. His name had been blackened and he was angry because whatever had happened wasn't his fault. He wanted John to clear his name.

'Find out and tell the truth,' he said.

As he said this I had a sensation of complete fury rushing through me. The ghost was in a blind rage that he had been blamed for something he didn't do.

'He knows,' he said, gesticulating at John. 'He knows.'

I asked the spirit why he had been scaring Katrina and the children and he said that he was trying to get John's attention. He wanted his name to be cleared and John was in a position to make sure that he wasn't unjustly blamed for the accident that had killed so many. He told me a name, 'Standford, Stampford, Stanfall ...' I murmured, trying to make it out exactly.

'Yes,' John said. 'Yes, that's the name.'

I also got the name 'Sarah', but neither John nor Katrina confirmed whether that meant anything to them.

By this time my energy was fading and I felt that the ghost had little else to say. I decided it was time to send him over. Eric came and the golden glow intensified in the room as he opened a spirit portal right next to me and I recited the De Profundis. The ghost moved across easily with Eric and in a matter of a few seconds the door closed and the golden snow that I had seen in the previous house, the week before, showered down in the room. It was beautiful.

I wiped my eyes and took a deep breath.

'Gone,' I pronounced as the light returned to normal.

John sat on the other side of the table, completely dazed. It turned out that he knew the area well. The housing estate where he lived had been built directly over the colliery which was now closed. John had also studied the area when he was at school and knew a lot of local history. The ghost had been completely right – John was in a good position to investigate what had really happened. For the first time during the haunting John had also experienced the ghost's presence – he had felt a pain on the left side of his body (right where the ghost was standing next to him) during the whole conversation I had conducted.

Katrina was delighted with the change in the atmosphere around her house. She could already sense it.

'It's definitely different in here,' she said.

I agreed. The room felt lighter now the presence was gone.

Katrina and I moved round the house, checking everywhere. We saved the boys' bedroom until last but it now felt like the children's room that it was. I was on a high, bouncing around, chatting to everyone. Sometimes that happens after a clearing – I may be able to feel the low atmosphere of a paranormal presence, but the up side of that is that I also feel the high of the change in atmosphere after it is gone. I was massively relieved, too, that my nerves over dinner hadn't been a premonition of a problem with the clearing.

I felt sorry for the ghost, even though he had been a malevolent presence for the family to live with. He had died a horrible, frightening death and had been held responsible for the deaths of countless other people. I hoped that John might indeed be able to get to the bottom of what had happened and put his soul completely to rest. For now, though, I was just so glad that it was all over.

At the front door Katrina gave me a big hug and thanked me again. Helping people, for me, really is the best bit of the job. It was lovely to see her so happy, her eyes shining, her troubles lifted away from her.

We drove back to the hotel and I fell into bed again. Two o'clock in the morning was beginning to feel early for me to get to sleep! I knew the next house was scheduled for only a few days' time.

'Better get my rest in,' I thought. 'I wonder where we're going.'

I lit one last cigarette before I turned in and I think I fell asleep half-dreaming about what might be for breakfast.

A couple of weeks later I rang the Elvins to make sure everything was OK. They had been to the local library to see if they could turn up any historical evidence that related to the ghost. Although there was definitely a mine where their house was built, it wasn't easy to find any details about accidents that may have happened there.

'I'm just glad the ghost has gone. We're really happy,' Katrina said. 'It's made such a difference. I feel like a different person, in fact!'

'It's best to get on with your lives now,' I replied.

This often happens after a clearing. Of course it would have been interesting to know some more historical fact, but the spirit was gone to his rest and the Elvins were back to normal. It's easy to want to know – to get caught up. But really, where it's possible, I think it's best for people just to get back to their normal lives.

Chapter Five

**The Hassett Family's House. Donnington.
Cleared on 9th September 2005.**

*The Hassetts have lived in their house for the last twenty years
and have experienced activity for most of that time. The paranormal phenomena they have experienced include noises
(bumping and banging), cold spots, voices and moving
objects. Members of the family have been touched and a
figure has been seen in one of the bedrooms. A large picture
inexplicably fell off the wall in the hallway, frightening the
family out of their wits. Neither the nail nor the cord on
the back of the picture were broken in any way. The cellar of
the house contains an old well and the family dogs will not go
near this part of the house.*

Be a Survivor, not a Victim

When I arrived at the train station in Leeds a few days later there was no one waiting to meet me. The weather had suddenly turned sunny after a couple of days of rain and the whole crew had rushed off to organize external shots of the house and interview the family while there was good light. I was becoming an old hand and reckoned I didn't need to be looked after so much. I spoke to Gemma on my mobile and then I hopped in a cab and made my own way to the hotel. Stepping onto the pavement at the other end I was pleasantly surprised. The Ramada Jarvis at Leeds in the Parkway was by far the nicest hotel we had stayed in since we started filming. I got into my room around four in the afternoon and realized that a lovely, long evening of room service, with a TV at the end of the bed, was stretched out before me. I ordered some mixed seafood and fries, a big salad and a plate of cheese and biscuits which, I reckoned would see me through the night as I could nibble away as much as I fancied. The last couple of hotels, if I'm honest, hadn't been so great and it was nice to settle in somewhere a bit more luxurious.

Around eight, having had a bath, read my book, eaten dinner and flicked through the TV channels, there was a knock on the door. Gemma was standing there with a bag of Diet Cokes.

'Thought you might like these,' she smiled and I invited her in.

'This is fantastic,' I said. 'The room is great. There is room service and everything.'

'Fancy popping down to the bar for a drink?' she suggested.

I grabbed my shoes, ran a brush through my hair and we went downstairs together. It was great to relax over a drink with Gemma, though we were both keen to get an early night for a change, so we didn't stay too long in the bar.

The next morning it was still sunny outside. We had been scheduled to start fairly late because we all knew we were going to be up all night. I had a leisurely breakfast in the dining room and met up with the crew as they appeared in dribs and drabs, sleepy-eyed. After everyone had gorged themselves on tea and toast and we had all shared the morning papers, I got a lift to the location. I didn't actually see the house for a long time as it was set back from the road. Michael turned up to do my hair and make-up in the Winnebago, which was parked off to one side and out of sight of the building.

'Do you feel anything yet?' Michael asked.

I didn't have any sensations about what might be going to happen.

'We're not near enough,' I pronounced. 'I've got to be in there.'

Once I was ready to go on camera, Gemma and Claire climbed into the Winnebago and said we should do the psychometry. They decided to use the seating area in the Winnebago for this.

'We might have to reshoot it anyway,' Gemma explained. 'Though we'll only have you saying what you picked up in the first place.'

What I always liked about September was that no one who worked there wanted to cheat and they were all very clear about that. I think that's so important on a show like *Haunted Homes*. Any psychic show, in fact. You can't allow any bluffs or second takes.

For the psychometry, Gemma and Claire brought in a box of items and set them out on the table with the usual thick red and gold cloth spread over the surface. I took a deep breath to centre myself and then I sat down, surveying the items one by one, but not touching them yet. When the cameras were ready I picked up the first object. It was an ornament of a sheepdog dressed like a shepherd with a crook in his paw. I felt the weight of the ornament in my palm and immediately had an image of extreme icy cold, the kind of atmosphere in which you can see your breath in the air. I saw that the ornament had been a present from a woman in her sixties and it had been given in the spirit of love. Next there was a handsome set of horse brasses mounted on a leather strap. As I picked it up

I could see a fireplace with open brickwork and a man who wasn't feeling well. I felt that the man had an arthritic knee, hip and back, and probably had a graze on the back of his hand. Again there was a sense of icy coldness as I touched this item. All this information was very specific and I wondered where it might fit in when I got into the house.

Next, I moved on to a prize cup which was engraved with the date 1902. As I touched it I could see open fields, way out in the countryside. Someone was shooting in the fields. Beside this on the table there were also a couple of photos in frames – one of a little boy, about two or three years old, and another of an older boy of around eight or nine with two women. I didn't pick up a huge amount from these photographs except that one of the two women was now dead and was a friendly ghost, who visited with a lot of love. There were also two pieces of jewellery – the first was a long gold chain with the figure of a cross-legged Buddha on the end of it. I could see that this was given as part of an anniversary celebration and it felt light and nice.

'Nothing in any way spooky about that one,' I said.

Last of all there was a ring with two white stones and one blue one. I had a sense from this item that the owner had unfinished business and needed to sort something out.

I was surprised. None of these objects felt tremendously heavy. More than anything I had a feeling of coldness from what I was handling, but nothing much more than that.

'Not too many paranormal clues here,' I said. Mostly, the items seemed to resonate with details of their owners, rather than details about the house. So far the haunting didn't feel that bad. I wasn't picking up any negative feelings other than the freezing sense I had of a very cold temperature. But there was no sense of fear from any of the objects, or any feeling that they had been thrown or moved.

'At last,' I thought, 'A gentle ghost.'

It wasn't what I had been expecting at all.

When the cameras stopped rolling Claire and Gemma started to pack things away and the crew said that next up I would go into the house and do my walk through.

The house was pretty old and we decided to film my arrival through the gates in a hire car. Then I could walk through the garden and up to the front door. As I drove through the gates I had my first sight of the house, which was a beautiful, old, stone-built semi-detached property. Its name was on the gates – Elmtree House – and as I drove through I thought what a lovely place it should be to live. The garden was well established with pretty flowers everywhere and now, at the end of the summer, the roses were still out and there was a lovely, fresh smell. I felt happy. I got out of the car and started to approach the building. As I got closer it seemed, clairvoyantly, that the house darkened as if there was a shadow over the place, and the happiness I felt shifted to uneasiness. The house had an air of expectation about it, as if it had taken a breath and not yet exhaled. In contrast with the psychometry, even before I opened the door I could tell that there was something very wrong here. The house seemed to be waiting.

As I pushed open the front door a wave of heaviness hit me. It was the same feeling that I had had in all the other properties: a sense of pressure in the air and, more than that this time, a feeling of depression too. Something very sad had happened here, I realized. Already I was picking up a feeling of acute discomfort and overwhelming sadness. It felt as if it had come unexpectedly, out of the blue. This was a lovely place and yet something was so very wrong.

I moved through the hallway and on to the living room where I felt immediately drawn to the fireplace. This was the fireplace I had seen when I picked up the horse brasses during the psychometry only a few minutes before. There was nothing burning in the grate (in fact, I learned later that no fire had been set there since the previous winter). Nonetheless, I could smell wood smoke and also the scent of flowers, perhaps roses. As I walked closer to the chimney breast I shivered at the extreme sense of icy cold. I think it was the worst cold spot I have ever sensed – and it was exactly what I had picked up from the dog ornament. Then I had the sudden image of an old woman in a rocking chair and an uneasy feeling turned in the pit of my stomach.

Moving on to the kitchen things felt even worse. For a start I had a sense of the room being out of shape and I felt uncomfortably constrained, as if the place was the wrong size and somehow didn't fit properly. It should have been bigger, I thought. Then I had a vision of barrels being rolled along the floor, as if Elmtree House had been a public house at some time. Yes, I could sense that there had been a lot of people here. It had been a busy place. But the room hadn't been like this at the time. It was much larger in those days. As I turned I could see a doorway and I knew instinctively that it led to a cellar. The kitchen had a very ominous air and the area around the cellar door felt particularly menacing. What came into my mind was that the cellar was like a pit from hell. I didn't go in there. Just the sight of the cellar door was shocking somehow. It was as if I had been punched in the chest. I had an overwhelming sense that I should leave. The place felt unbearably threatening and my body was going into overdrive. My heart was racing and there was panic pulsing through me. It was some adrenalin rush.

'I have to get out of here,' I breathed. 'Now.'

I walked away, trying to control the urge to run – that wouldn't have looked very professional on camera. I was shaking and my skin came up in goosebumps. Then, like the feeling I had when I approached the house, I felt a sense of dread, of fearful expectation, although this time it was extremely strong, to the point that it was overpowering. I had to sit down. Outside, someone brought me a drink of water and I gathered my thoughts.

'If this is what I feel like at the entrance to the cellar, what is it going to be like down there?' I wondered.

The atmosphere inside the house was awful – certainly I hadn't picked up anything like this from the items in the Winnebago. It took me a few minutes to find my feet again before I felt I could go back and face it. The crew were hanging around waiting for me and I felt guilty about that.

'Right,' I said. 'Let's go into the cellar.' I tried to sound cheery but I was frightened. 'Something terrible has happened here,' I said. I could feel it.

It was difficult to walk down the steps. As I got deeper underground the air felt heavier and heavier. It was like walking into a swamp. Like the kitchen upstairs I knew that the cellar had also been much larger originally. Things had been altered here, but it was as if the building itself remembered what it had been like originally. There were visual echoes of it. And the feeling in the cellar was very uncomfortable – a sadness, but a frantic kind of sadness. To one side, encircled by a low raised wall, there was what looked like an old well that reached down further than I could see. I had a terrible feeling about the whole area. Something very bad had happened there. Then suddenly, like an abrupt and horrible shock, I could see that there had been bodies laid out in this room. They were bloody and had died a murderous death. Mostly they were men, but there was one woman that I could see. It had been a massacre – something dreadful.

'I have to go up now,' I said, trying to stay calm, but my heart was hammering in my chest and I felt sick. I had to get out of there as fast as I could.

'This cellar is the epicentre,' I said when I was upstairs again, and the relief of being away from it seeped through my senses.

I took a few moments to find my feet once more and then realized that there were a lot of other rooms to look at. I was just glad to be out of that hole in the ground. I set off for the second public room and as I stepped over the door jamb I once more had a sense of the atmosphere being icy cold and of the room now looking different from its original incarnation. Like elsewhere in the house, this room too had been a busy place and I could sense footsteps and the noise and chatter of a crowd of people. However, although the air pressure felt heavy, it didn't even touch the sense of pressure and unpleasantness of the cellar.

I went back out into the hallway and up the stairs. Here the atmosphere lightened up even further. There had definitely been spirit activity all over the house but further away from the epicentre it was more an overspill than anything else and the ambience was far more pleasant. On the stairs I felt that footsteps had been heard, but nothing much more than that. In the guest bedroom I had a strong sense that a figure had been seen in the doorway. Then in the main bedroom I could tell that someone had been touched on the face and that, again, something had been seen in the doorway and in the mirror on the wardrobe. In the third bedroom I didn't sense any activity at all – the room was occupied by the family's energetic parrot that was flapping around at all the excitement he could hear as we filmed around the rest of the house.

'Phew. I'm glad that is over,' I breathed as I walked back down the stairs, diagnosis complete.

I couldn't imagine living in such a strained atmosphere. Elmtree House felt as if it was being pulled out on a wire. Very sad. Very tense. And very, very heavy. I knew that the family must have been badly affected by what had been going on. Living in such a strained environment on a day-to-day basis would be difficult. I felt sorry for them.

'I definitely need a cup of tea,' I announced and Gemma went off to see if she could find one for me, appearing with a steaming mug a couple of minutes later. I took it outside and had a few quiet moments in the garden to recover. The sun was shining and there were bees bobbing up and down along the flower beds. From my vantage point in the garden, the house looked idyllic.

Gemma called me from the door.

'The family are here. They're ready,' she said.

I gulped down the last of my tea and went to meet them.

Phil and Theresa Hassett were sitting on the sofa in the living room with their grown-up daughter, Pippa. Both Theresa and her daughter had cheeky faces, with darting eyes, and although they looked nervous I thought that they would be good fun to be around. Phil was an engineer, a dark-haired, square-faced man who had a strong presence about him and felt very solid. They were a happy family, I could see. Pippa no longer lived at home and neither did her sister (who wasn't around) but both girls had had many paranormal experiences in the house. Theresa and Phil could hardly restrain themselves from telling me stories of what they had experienced and letting me know that recently the activity seemed to have heightened.

I told them what I had seen in the cellar and about my sense that the house had been larger.

'It was,' said Theresa.

It turned out that there had been a structural defect in the house and part of the front had collapsed some years before. This had been rebuilt and the house, which had originally been an inn, had been converted into two separate family homes. The cellar, now the epicentre of the haunting, had been split in two and in the house next door this area had been filled in. Theresa and Phil had a friend who had gone down the well on a rope. He had brought plenty of rope with him, but couldn't find where the well led to, because it was so deep.

The kitchen and other downstairs rooms had originally been far larger, too, but were now split and used on both sides of the conversion.

'I knew there was something strange going on before I moved in here,' Theresa said. 'I could hear voices. Everyone said I was doolally.'

In fact, all the family had heard voices over the years – the babble of a crowd – the kind of noise that comes from a busy pub. There was nothing distinct that they could make out, no particular phrases, only the noise of people chatting away.

'That's not a haunting,' I explained. 'That is just a memory. It's like a video rerun of what used to go on here. You can't interact with it. However, you do have a ghost here and that is what is causing your problems.'

Phil told me that a couple of weeks before he had seen a black shadow in his bedroom. He thought it was a burglar and had jumped out of bed but the shape had disappeared and there was nothing there. It had scared the living daylights out of him.

'I would like to know what it is,' Theresa said. 'At first I thought maybe I was just a bit weird because I was seeing these things, or feeling these things.'

'Don't worry,' I said, although the truth was that I was worried myself. I wasn't looking forward to the feel of that cellar at night. I wanted to reassure the family, though, and no matter what, I wanted to get rid of whatever was plaguing this lovely building. 'Whatever happens I won't leave until your house is clear of this,' I promised.

'Back to normal in here would be nice,' Theresa smiled.

'So, will you stay and do the vigil with me? I'll be here,' I said.

The Hassetts all agreed.

I went to sit down in the Winnebago while Chris and Mark went to have their walk around the house and the crew set up the cameras for the evening. Mark was also putting in his usual ghost busting equipment which he centred around the kitchen and the cellar area. Around seven o'clock Gemma came in and said that there was a nice Italian restaurant down the road where we could have some dinner. She had booked a table for fifteen, so we wandered down there with the Hassetts and ordered some pasta. Halfway through the meal, Pippa began to feel very hot and unwell. She went white and decided to leave and go outside to try to recover. I didn't feel it was a good idea for someone to come on the vigil if they weren't feeling quite right and after a short chat we decided that Pippa should get a medical check up, just to be sure that she was all right, and not come back to Elmtree House until after we'd finished. It's one thing someone feeling nervous or unwell during the course of the vigil, but I didn't like to think about what would happen to someone who was feeling ill before we even started, so Pippa bowed out.

We got back to the house when it was getting dark. It was quite late and we decided to start the vigil in the living room beside the fireplace. Mark and I were to join Theresa and Phil, and we set up some high-backed chairs around the grate. We were all nervous. Theresa's eyes were darting around the room as I gave my talk about being careful and using torches. I was concerned that the cellar steps were steep and slightly rough and I didn't like the idea of anyone getting panicky and falling.

'Be sure to use your torch. And remember that whatever happens it can't really harm you,' I said. 'It's just scary.'

Around midnight the last member of the crew gave me the thumbs up as they left. Theresa, Phil, Mark and I were left in the locked-down house. I did feel slightly anxious even before we started. After what I had seen in the cellar in the daytime I wondered what might happen now it was dark. I was about to find out. We counted three – two – one and the lights went out.

As my eyes adjusted to the darkness I could hear stones falling down the chimney and into the grate. That isn't unusual, except that outside there wasn't a breath of wind.

'And it's a sealed chimney,' Theresa said.

The Hassetts had had the top of it capped some time before.

The stones were quite large and were now bouncing off the top of the metal wood-burning stove in the fireplace. We sat for a while listening to them, wondering where on earth they might be coming from. Then I suggested that Mark and I should go upstairs. I thought we might as well spend some time in each of the less affected rooms in the house before heading down to the cellar.

'Do you mind staying downstairs while we go and have a look?' I asked.

The Hassetts agreed.

As I climbed the stairs and crossed the upstairs hallway I could feel a tingling all over my body. It was a strange, slightly surreal sensation. Mark and I went into the main bedroom and sat on either side of the bed. Mark leant forward.

'I think I can see something. A figure,' he said. 'Just coming around the door.'

I didn't see this myself, though I did think that the door moved slightly.

Both of us sat in the bedroom for a while. I think we were both reticent because we knew that when we went downstairs it would be time to go into the cellar. Trepidation played around my stomach, which was turning over at the thought of having to go back down into that murderous, heavy atmosphere. We sat in the bedroom until we couldn't put it off any longer.

Back downstairs the Hassetts had had their own experiences in the living room. Theresa had seen a shadow while Phil had seen something he described as 'smoke by the TV'.

While this activity was interesting we knew what we had to do and Mark and I both volunteered to go down to the cellar and see what might be going on there.

As I stood at the door I felt slightly sick. The rooms upstairs were pitch dark, but looking into the cellar there was a strange, inky blackness that filled me with even more foreboding.

We took the steps sideways, very slowly, because they were so steep and so narrow. Normally in a dark house you can still see the outline of the person next to you but in the cellar I really couldn't make out a thing. I couldn't even tell which way I was facing once we were there. Mark simply disappeared. We used our torches on the stairs for safety but when we got down we switched them off. After only a moment in the all-encompassing, pitch blackness I felt as if I was drowning. A panic began to rise in my chest and I had to concentrate hard on my breathing to be able to control it. I could hear small stones falling, just like upstairs. I wondered if that had something to do with the well which was situated in the middle of the room, but the noise didn't seem to be coming from there. We could also hear footsteps right above us, although later, when we investigated, it turned out that we were directly beneath a room which wasn't being used for the programme and was locked. I jumped as I heard a sharp intake of breath next to my left ear, though I didn't feel any air moving at all.

'Woah!' I shouted.

I have a lot of experience but the cellar in Elmtree House was really freaking me out. The atmosphere was too intense.

'Settle down,' Mark tried to soothe me.

I concentrated on my breathing again to calm myself, but my heart rate was soaring. There were more noises, like little clicks, and the sound of more little stones falling.

Suddenly Mark yelled. It really gave me a jolt.

'Something poked me,' he complained.

He had felt it in his side, a sharp pain under his ribs. It was very sore. We waited another couple of minutes and I worried that I was going to get too disorientated. I really felt that I had had enough.

'Maybe we should go up,' I suggested. 'I don't want to be poked.'

'Let's give it a bit more time,' Mark said.

We waited. It was icy cold and there was a constant stream of strange noises. The horrible feeling I had in my chest continued. I kept thinking that my eyes would get used to the dark but even after several minutes there was no difference to when I first came down. I couldn't make out a thing. I felt completely claustrophobic. It was difficult to control and my instincts, much as they had been during the day, were to bolt. After a few more minutes we turned on our torches again and I began to feel slightly easier. I asked Mark to show me where he had been hurt and sure enough there was a red mark on his skin which looked as if it was still sore.

'Come on,' I said. 'Time's up.'

I can't tell you how glad I was to get out of that place.

Upstairs I sat down for a few moments to centre myself. I knew that I would have to go back down into the cellar soon. It was important for the family that they should experience the haunting properly, one last time, at its very worst. Mark took Phil outside to watch on the monitors while I managed to persuade Theresa to come downstairs with me. I was feeling slightly sick by this time and had a strong aversion to returning to what felt to me like a death pit, but I knew it was for the best and I struggled hard against my feelings.

'If anything happens, just call up,' Angelo, the director, told us.

'Thanks,' I said half-heartedly. It wasn't that I particularly felt something was going to happen. But just being in the heavy, dense atmosphere was so unpleasant that I just didn't want to do it any more.

We switched on our torches at the top of the stairs and slowly descended. As the lights went off when we reached the bottom we could hear the tapping noises again and the falling gravel. Then Theresa suddenly grabbed my arm.

'I can see something,' she said. 'A being. There.'

We both shouted out and I switched my torch back on. Theresa couldn't find her torch anywhere. It had moved five feet from where she had left it to the other side of the dank well that was situated next to us. It wasn't possible for Theresa to have pushed it. I had felt for myself that both her hands had been on my arm. I switched the torch off again and we decided to give it a bit more time. The small noises continued and Theresa said that she was getting a headache and felt ill. I wasn't feeling great either. It wasn't much later that we decided to climb the stairs and make our way out.

I was glad to get out of the house and lit up a cigarette as soon as I hit the outside air.

'Blimey,' I said. 'That was pretty heavy.'

I chain-smoked two in a row before I even thought about getting into the Winnebago. Theresa and I settled down, both relieved to be back among other people. The atmosphere had lifted completely and I began to relax as the crew bantered cheerfully, eating biscuits and getting on with their jobs. This time it was our turn to watch on the monitor, though the boys elected to go upstairs to the bedroom where Mark thought he had seen something peering around the door earlier. They weren't going anywhere near the cellar.

'On the monitor it looks really light,' I commented. 'You can hardly see in there. Those cameras are amazing.'

I was cross with myself that I had panicked so badly. Although I had had a couple of jumpy moments in other houses during the series, I really just wanted to run away from Elmtree House. I was thankful to be out of there, but still annoyed that I had lost my cool. It occurred to me that I had had the same feelings as someone who wasn't psychic. I'd just had the experience of what it is like for someone on the other side of the fence. Someone who is scared. It really made me appreciate what people go through when they face a paranormal encounter.

Theresa and I settled down in the Winnebago and watched Mark and Phil sitting on the bed. Nothing happened in the bedroom.

'They should try the cellar,' I said.

Then Chris the sceptic thought that he should really go and take a look. I think the fact that the house had affected me so badly intrigued him. He wandered from room to room and even braved the cellar on his own, although once again I don't think he ever turned off his torch. He said he felt disoriented but then it was so dark that he felt that for him, darkness was the only cause.

Everyone had had enough and it was after four in the morning when we finished. The crew began to dismantle the equipment and I got a lift back to the hotel.

'Don't worry about this,' I said to Phil and Theresa. 'Tomorrow I will find out what it is all about.'

'I'm just glad that you're here,' Theresa smiled. 'I thought I was going mad.'

I did feel sorry for the Hassetts as I drove away. They were going back into that house and they were going to be left there alone for the rest of the night.

I sat up for a while and chain-smoked by the window in my hotel room until exhaustion overtook me.

'I suppose it's good, isn't it, Eric? Feeling what other people feel will make me understand things better.'

'Not a bad idea,' he agreed.

My heart rate was finally back to normal, but I still felt tense about the next day. I didn't want to really lose it, especially in front of the cameras. I had come close to that earlier in the evening, I knew. I'm quite a proud kind of person, really, and besides, I felt it was my job to be the brave one. I also felt responsible. The ghost had poked Mark hard and his skin would be red for days. What happened if it pushed someone?

'I have to keep a grip,' I told myself. 'This spirit is going over.'

And I stubbed out my cigarette and got into bed.

The next morning there was a slightly bashful atmosphere among the crew. Everyone met for sandwiches just before midday and they were teasing each other about getting scared. Some of the crew had admitted the night before that they thought they had seen things. One guy had smelt wood smoke, just as I had when I first entered the house. There was a large group of us and we lazed around the hotel dining room for ages, waiting until it was time for the next part of filming to start. The others were making guesses as to the cause of the haunting.

'I bet it's a fire. That's what the wood smoke is about,' one guy said.

All eyes turned to me, as if for an explanation.

'I don't know,' I said. 'I'm not switched on. I was as scared as anyone last night.'

When the sandwiches were done we headed over to the house. Phil and Theresa told us they had scarcely slept. They were looking pale and tired all right. The crew set up interviews to catch reactions about the night before and everyone was soon busy, scurrying about on the set. I sat in the garden and tried to gather my thoughts. I was nervous about the clearing and went through a long series of 'what ifs'. What if this is the day I can't sort it? What if something goes wrong?

Early in the evening we decided to set up for the clearing, which inevitably was going to be in the cellar. The stairs were steep and narrow and the space was slightly awkward, with the well making it impossible to use part of the room.

'A logistical nightmare,' one of the production assistants said.

'Yeah. We'll manage it though,' someone else replied.

There was a nice old pub nearby and some of us went for dinner, leaving the rest to set up the cameras. I tucked into some leek and potato soup and lovely fishcakes while we chatted around the table.

'What's great is that you're here and you believe us,' Theresa said.

I felt that it was important that we were bringing events like this to the attention of the public. It should help people to feel more confident about discussing spiritual issues. Hauntings aren't everywhere, but it must be dreadful when your house is haunted and you can't talk about it to anyone; when you don't know where to go for help. The experience of being thoroughly spooked the day before had given me fresh empathy with people who have to deal with hauntings alone and out of their depth.

We drove back to the house where the cellar had been all set up. Everything was ready. I can't say I was truly looking forward to going down there again, but at least I knew this would be the last time. Coming down the stairs the

place did look amazing, though the heavy feeling persisted. There were candles in all the alcoves and a small table had been set up with three chairs around it and more candles spread on top. I decided to sit in the middle, between Theresa and Phil. It was going to be difficult to concentrate, I realized. I just didn't like this place. It felt all wrong.

'At least I am going to use my psychic power this time,' I thought. I had a flicker of curiosity because I wanted to know what had really gone on here.

'It's going to be grim, though,' I decided. 'Best just get on with it.'

As I sat down the room fell silent. The crew were backed up against the walls and the candles were flickering, casting a warm light over the whole cellar. I explained that I was going to search the house psychically for the ghost and bring it back to this place, ask as many questions as I could and then send it over.

'Hang in, whatever happens,' I said. 'Just stay calm.'

I think I was speaking as much to myself as to anyone else.

'I am going to start now.'

I closed my eyes, took a deep breath and began. First, I left my body and walked up into the kitchen. The ghost wasn't anywhere to be seen. I continued through the other ground floor rooms but couldn't see anything, so I decided to climb the stairs to the bedroom floor. Up there I went from room to room but there was no ghost at all. This worried me. What if, after all this, I couldn't find it? I came back down into the cellar and just as I was about to announce that there wasn't a ghost around today, a man walked straight through the cellar wall.

He was wearing a hooded cloak with a motif on the front in the shape of a plant. This meant at first that I couldn't see his face. He seemed thin, though, and as he walked around the room I caught glimpses under his hood. His face was gaunt and he had high cheekbones and very pale skin. His eyes were large and a beautiful brown colour, although he had a despairing expression on his face as if his eyes had glazed over. All of a sudden I felt that I was being bombarded by images. This ghost didn't speak in words, he only communicated with me visually.

I could see the cellar, much larger, as it had originally been. There were iron manacles on the walls and when he had been here, alive, the ghost had prisoners that he was in charge of. These people were chained up and I could see him, as a man, checking that they were secured. The group were only in the cellar for one night. They were travelling – a journey from north to south – and he was in charge, travelling with them. Then I saw three men coming down the stairs. They murdered the prisoners, massacring them with their swords. The prisoners didn't have a chance. There were four or five men and one woman and they all died. The ghost had come down the stairs and when he saw what was going on, he ran to get help. Upstairs he had found a man who was sleeping, but he didn't manage to rouse him. He knew he should go down and defend the prisoners, but he didn't. Instead he hid. He was ashamed of that. Later, the men came upstairs to find him and they killed him anyway.

The ghost's name was Samuel but his surname was unclear to me. It sounded like Aldridge or Albridge. He had been travelling from the Scottish border some time in the 1820s. I had an image of an iron box which was tied with metal straps. The box contained money and the men who murdered the party had stolen it. I didn't understand the connection. There seemed to be no reason why they would have to have killed everyone in order to take the box, but that is what I saw, so I said it.

It was clear to me that this ghost was tormented by his guilt. He knew he should have fought the attackers and he felt awful about running away and leaving his charges to die. He said his murderers had been found and hanged, but that didn't make him feel any better. He had been a coward. Then he showed me an image of a church nearby. In the graveyard there had been bodies that had been moved – they had originally been buried in a pit.

By now I was feeling exhausted. This was a long and emotionally draining story. The dreadful feeling in the cellar seemed entirely understandable to me now. This man had let himself and his charges down, he had been tormented by his own inaction, and there seemed no way he could ever repent enough for what had happened. Dreadful murders had taken place here. Those people had been defenceless, chained to the walls. They had been slaughtered horribly. Such a vicious and cold-blooded act would leave an imprint of its own, never mind that someone had witnessed it, done nothing and then been slaughtered too.

I felt it was time to send Samuel to his rest. I asked Eric to open the doorway and he appeared immediately beside me. Then, in the cellar wall, right behind Samuel, an opening like a doorway showed itself. Samuel seemed to be sucked into it. He went over easily and I began to say the De Profundis. I was feeling high emotions – in fact, I was crying – and I found it difficult to gasp for breath. Though Samuel was gone, the door remained and the feeling in the room was as if it was a vacuum, as if all the awful feelings were being sucked out of the place and it was being cleared. I was gasping for air and halfway through I had to stop speaking. I carried on with the De Profundis in my head even though I couldn't form the words aloud, and managed to get out the last line of it. As I said the final word the door closed and Eric disappeared. I was shaking.

It took several minutes before I was able to speak again. I had lost control of myself and was taken up with emotions – an uneasy mixture of sadness and relief and simply feeling overcome. When I had calmed down Theresa told me that bodies had been moved nearby. A nursery school was being built and some kind of burial pit had been discovered. One of the researchers said she would look into it. Theresa was smiling, but she wanted to be sure that her house was now cleared of any ghostly activity.

'Is it definitely gone?' she asked.

'Yes,' I said. 'Can't you feel it?'

We went for a walk around the house to check. The place felt almost breezy and very, very light. Theresa couldn't believe it.

'Thank you so much,' she said.

I was glad to have been able to help and I reminded myself that although it had been difficult and heavy, this spirit had been tortured rather than evil. I gratefully took a mug of tea from Gemma and sat on the sofa while the cameras were dismantled. There was a festive air around the house because I think here, almost everyone had felt the haunting for themselves and it was lovely that the place felt so much better.

Then the Hassetts' other daughter, Debbie, arrived.

'Don't you remember?' she said to her parents. 'When we moved in there were iron stays in the walls of the cellar. We moved them.'

'That's right,' said Phil. 'There were.'

'Well, you've got a clean house now. Enjoy it,' I said.

I was pleased for the Hassetts, that after everything they had been through they could finally have their house back. It must have been a tremendous relief for them. After a haunting that heavy it takes a while to settle down. But I knew the Hassetts would be fine. They had known all along that their home had been a public house, and I heard that the researcher at September had tried to find a listing in historical records, but had come up with nothing. I just hoped that the Hassetts would let it go. I don't think it does anyone any good to become too obsessive about the past. I now felt confident that the spirit was at rest, which was the most important thing for all concerned.

Around two in the morning we drove back to the hotel and I thought I was going to sleep for a week. I was so relieved that my body had turned to jelly and I felt completely relaxed. I almost fell through the bedroom door, climbed into my nightie and under the covers and then, wouldn't you know it, there was a party going on in the room next door. I could hear music through the wall behind my head and there was no way I was going to manage to sleep through it.

'Eric,' I called out in exasperation.

'I don't know what you're asking *me* for,' he laughed. 'I'm not magical, you know.'

I leant over to the phone and called the reception desk, who sent someone up to sort it out.

When the music was turned down and the noisy voices calmed I turned over and closed my eyes. I don't think it even took me a minute to drift off to sleep. The last thing I remember was wondering whatever might be coming my way next.

Chapter Six

*The Stevenses have lived in their house for a while but it is
only in the last two years that the family have experienced
paranormal activity. The phenomena they report include
orbs, noises, a female voice, cold spots and electrical disturbances. The family have discovered buried bones in the
garden. There is a stain on one of the walls which has been
painted over, but light appears from the wall in any photographs taken of it. A female figure has been seen on the upper
floor. All the Stevenses' family and friends refuse to stay in
the house.*

You Are Never Alone

After the luxurious surroundings of the hotel in Leeds I had secret hopes that the standard of accommodation was on the rise. However, when I arrived in Lincolnshire by train and got a taxi to the hotel where the whole team was booked in, my heart sank. It was a cheerless place that smelt of damp. My room was dingy and on the chilly side. I wasn't looking forward to spending an evening there on my own before my segments of the filming started the next day but I didn't have many options.

'Oh well,' I thought, 'it can't always be the Ritz.'

I was hungry so I went downstairs and ordered what turned out to be an inedible meal in the restaurant. I had chosen pie and chips, but the whole thing was so greasy that I couldn't stomach it and after a couple of mouthfuls I went back upstairs, chatted on the phone to my daughter for a while and then watched television with my feet up until I fell asleep. I was beginning to feel homesick –

I hadn't been back for a while and I wanted to see my family and my friends and wake up in my own bedroom.

The next morning I was feeling very indulgent. It had been the best night's sleep I had had for ages, and after reading the paper and having some toast and eggs, I went back up to bed and had another couple of hours' sleep. I had put my 'Do Not Disturb' sign on the door but was woken from my nap by a maid in an old-fashioned black and white uniform who came into the room to clean it. She said sorry and left the room again when she saw that I was still in bed, but as I surfaced into consciousness I had to wonder at this hotel having such smartly dressed housekeeping staff. It seemed incongruous and I wasn't sure if the maid had in fact been real or not. Perhaps this was a dream relating to the house I was going to, or perhaps a spirit which visited the hotel. However, later, when I came back upstairs from lunch my mind was put to rest when I saw the maids clearing their trolleys in the hallway. All of them were wearing the same uniform and, out of place or not, they were definitely alive and well.

'Easy to get carried away,' I thought. 'I have an imagination as well as a gift.'

I have never in my life done so much mediumship work all at once. When someone is pregnant, suddenly they notice that everyone has babies or babies on the way. Likewise, because everything I had been doing for weeks was about the spirit world, I realized that I was beginning to assume that the spirit world was everywhere.

'That's no good,' I told myself. 'It shouldn't be my first conclusion.'

After lunch, Linda from the production team knocked on my door and went through what I was going to wear. I had brought a white kaftan top, but we decided on reflection that it would most likely become see-through on camera so we chose a light blue shirt and I decided to wear a white vest underneath it, just in case.

Linda took me to another room in the hotel which had been hired for the psychometry and once I had fixed my make up we got underway. The room was decked with candles, which Gemma and Claire had laid out to make it look more atmospheric.

'You two are demons for atmosphere,' I said.

The place looked pretty good. Much nicer than the room I was staying in.

Laid out on a table with a red cloth over it there were several objects. I sat down, nodded at the cameraman so he would start shooting and picked up the first. I chose a gold chain with a Saint Christopher medal on it as the first item, because it seemed the kind of thing that might have some strong feelings about it. I had a sense that it had been worn a lot. An image came into my mind of around fifty years ago, of a terraced house with outhouses. I thought it had belonged to someone's grandmother. I got no sense of the haunting but knew there was a lot of love in this family.

Next, there was a pair of cufflinks that were gold with oval mother of pearl insets. These had belonged to two men, one handing them down to the other, and were only worn occasionally and kept for special occasions.

After that there was a diamond solitaire ring that looked like it could be an engagement ring.

'Is this a red herring?' I thought.

It seemed too obvious that it was an engagement ring but when I picked it up I decided that it was, and that the woman who wore this ring was stressed and agitated about something other than her relationship. In fact, all the relationships I was picking up were very strong and stable. The trouble in this family came from outside and although it was affecting them badly there was enough love there to see them through the crisis.

After that there were two photographs in decorative gold frames. One was black and white and was of an elderly couple with a toddler. The other was a sepia shot of the same boy, only older. The boy in the photographs was still part of the family but the older couple were now in spirit, and again I had the sense of a very close family link and a lot of love between these people.

I chose a silver charm bracelet next – it was very pretty, with a sweet violin charm and also a tiny bottle hanging from the chain. I felt the bracelet had a connection to the grandmother of the family. I could smell a flowery, old-fashioned face powder and knew that the old lady was dead but that the bracelet had been worn for a long time and often, and that it had been passed on to someone else after she died.

From a row of three medals I sensed that one of them had been awarded because a man had carried another man out of trouble. He had gone into a roofless building in order to save the other fellow and this had been extremely dangerous. He had flashbacks all his life about what he had done and he had suffered from dreadful nightmares. He was a very brave man, though. A hero. It is often possible to get very strong images from medals and I knew that this person had been part of the family I was going to and that the love of the family had sustained him through his difficulties.

Lastly, there was a silver crucifix on a white ribbon. This was used for protection and was kept near a bed. It was needed by the people who owned it and had been blessed by a priest.

'There is fear in the household, but a lot of love,' I summed up, recognizing as I said it that it was a haunted house and of course there was going to be a lot of fear.

I laid the last item down again and sat back in my chair. I realized that I was hungry. So far everything I'd had in the hotel restaurant had been pretty horrible, and I had only picked at what was on the plate.

'There's a pub down the road,' Claire suggested. 'I think they do burgers.'

'Have we got time?' I asked.

Claire grinned. 'We'll make it,' she said.

We raced off down the road and got our order in.

I felt a lot better after I had eaten something. Claire drove me to the house, and the crew were already setting up inside. From the street I felt it looked just like a house a kid would draw – it was very square and regular and opened straight onto the pavement. Outside I didn't have any strong sense of what might be inside. We fixed my hair and make up and then one of the crew told me that they were ready for me to begin. I took a deep breath and pushed open the front door.

Inside I immediately felt extremely cold and very uneasy. The first room I went into was the living room.

It was a very light and bright room with a cream carpet and a comfortable-looking burgundy sofa. There was an open fireplace with a cast-iron stove inset and, just like at Elmtree House, I could smell wood smoke here although the stove had not been used all summer. From the living room I thought that there had definitely been noises heard from the stairwell in the hall. I moved on into the dining room which was next door. The ceiling in there was lower than the other room and it felt as if the room was the wrong shape, but I couldn't sense anything wrong psychically. The paranormal activity here was low; it was only that the room was a different shape from what it had been originally, and that felt uncomfortable. I could see that there had been renovations carried out on the house. There were places where the family hadn't finished decorating yet. But these renovations had been more than cosmetic – the shape of these rooms had changed.

Coming back through the living room I was shocked to see the apparition of a female spirit by the fireplace. She was wearing a white flowing gown. I had not opened up fully on purpose and was very surprised to see this ghost. In fact, I deliberately turned away because I didn't want to make contact with her. If I had done so and she needed to be cleared it wouldn't have been right to keep her in the house and I would have had to send her over. I just turned my eyes in the opposite direction. When I looked towards the fireplace once more she had disappeared. I felt a temperature drop and the room was suddenly chilly.

Going up the stairs I didn't sense anything but as I came out onto the landing I had the strong sense of the shape of the house again being very different from the way it had originally been built. It felt to me as if the place was slightly distorted and there were two realities constantly battling it out there. I decided to concentrate on the way it was now.

From the hallway there were two bedrooms, one on each side. To the right there was a boy's room with a sloping ceiling and I sensed no activity in this room except that something might have been seen around the doorway.

On the other side was the adults' room. As I walked in I immediately knew that there had been more activity in here than on the other side of the hall. The person on the left-hand side of the bed couldn't sleep and had been agitated by paranormal activity in the room through the night. I knew that paranormal occurrences had been witnessed between the bed and the window in the room and also in the doorway. The feeling in the doorway was particularly uncomfortable and I sensed that the door had been closed to block out the sight of something that the person in the room had not wanted to see.

Moving on there was a pretty, pink, girl's bedroom and here, again, there had been quite a bit of paranormal activity with sightings between the bed and the window and in the doorway. What was disturbing me as I moved on through the bedrooms was that I couldn't sense an epicentre – the activity seemed to be everywhere. In fact, the strongest sensation I had was the feeling that the house should be a completely different shape. That feeling was almost overwhelming. It was odd – a strange sensation of things being ill-fitting as if I had put on a pair of trousers I expected to be a skirt. The old layout of rooms seemed to be trying to re-establish itself and I felt that probably this ghost could see the new configuration of rooms and was very confused by them. In fact, confusion was the keynote of what I sensed. There was a lot of bewilderment.

'At least this one seems lower key,' I said, because I hadn't felt the dreadful sadness or heavy, heavy fear that I had experienced in the last few houses. It was unusual that this was a female spirit – far less serious hauntings seem to be by women ghosts in my experience – and I did feel that although this was a troublesome, strong spirit I didn't have the sense of fear and foreboding which had accompanied some of the other paranormal activity I had experienced over the past few weeks.

Downstairs, Bob and Shelley Stevens were in the living room. Shelley was a pretty woman with shoulder-length blonde hair and Bob was a dark, centred guy who, I guessed, was the child in the photographs I had handled earlier. This certainly was a family held together by a strong sense of love and devotion to each other and the haunting had affected both of the Stevenses badly.

'I have seen the spirit already,' I told them, 'which is very unusual. I am not fully open yet. This is a strong one and that means she might be difficult to control.'

They were both relieved that I had seen the woman – although both of them had also seen a female apparition they weren't confident that it was she who was haunting the house. Bob was deeply affected by the fact that I had already seen the ghost and I could see that he was moved and almost crying. I think having his own suspicions and experiences confirmed meant a lot to him.

'Don't worry,' I said. 'We'll do the vigil this evening and that will be the last time you will spend a night with this ghost in your home.'

I went on to talk about the cold spots, the smell of smoke and the sense I had that the house should be a different shape. It turned out that the changes to the layout in the house had been extensive, particularly upstairs, and this tied in with the sense I had when I walked around. Bob explained that at one time there had been a long hallway or corridor which was no longer there. This, I felt, might be the key to the problem. The spirit was unsettled, perhaps looking for something, and very confused that she couldn't even find her way around her own house. It must have been awful for her. The spirit wasn't looking for attention or trying to scare the family; I knew that she was only mystified and disturbed by something she didn't understand.

Then Shelley confirmed that she was the one who slept on the left in their bed and that she had been agitated on several occasions, as I had sensed when I had been in the bedroom. Other visitors to the house had also experienced disturbed nights due to the ghost's activities.

'People won't come and stay any more,' Shelley told me. So many of the Stevenses' friends had had bad experiences in the house that they didn't want to visit overnight. This spirit had also moved objects. During the renovation work tools had gone missing, only to be found later in sealed boxes of kitchen equipment that had been stored away. Furniture had moved too.

'Mostly it seems to happen around holidays – Easter and Christmas – but recently it's happening all the time and there haven't been any special holidays,' Bob told me.

It had clearly been very unsettling and frightening for the family, though I suspected that the activity was there most of the time and it was only when they were on holiday and spending more time at home that the family noticed what was going on.

'Have you seen her?' I asked Shelley.

'Yes. In the bedroom upstairs. More than once. She needs sorting out,' Shelley said. 'She scares me.'

'It'll be over soon,' I promised. 'I won't leave until she's gone.'

Chris and Mark had arrived by this time for their walk through and I went outside and smoked, chatting to some of the crew while Bob and Shelley showed the others around. Then the long process of setting up infrared cameras and Mark's ghost busting equipment started.

It was already dark by the time we were ready to eat. Claire suggested a nice pub nearby and when she phoned and explained they kindly agreed to keep their kitchens open for us, although they usually stopped serving food by this time. We booked a table for fourteen and went straight over.

By the time we got back to the house it was close to midnight and everything was ready. I gave my now usual talk about keeping safe, always using torches for going up and down the stairs and not panicking. I took my time. It's important always to remember that although I had given this speech before and the crew had heard it a number of times, this evening we were there for the Stevenses and for them, all this was new.

The last of the crew piled outside and Bob, Shelley, Mark and I were alone. We decided to sit in the living room in a semi circle on the floor. Mark nodded to me just before the lights went out and then we were plunged into darkness. It was a full moon that night but blackout curtains had been put up at the windows and my eyes adjusted slowly.

My first sense was that the room was becoming increasingly cold. I could feel a sharp breeze on my legs and all down my right-hand side. Bob said that he could feel this too, although we both knew that there was nowhere this could feasibly have come from and it wasn't a cold night outside. Bob said this had happened before in the house. His daughter's bedroom had always been freezing and there hadn't seemed to be anything they could do about it. The room had only heated up after he had asked the chaplain from his work to come and bless the house. Now the sense of coldness was coming and going, rather than being fixed in one place. I was shivering.

Then suddenly Mark said, 'I can see a figure. Through there.'

I looked in the direction of the dining room but couldn't make out anything myself. Mark was fascinated, though. Bob could see a strange triangle of light which couldn't have come from outside because of the thick blackouts that had been put up. There seemed to be light anomalies all over the ground floor – one person seeing one of them, and someone else seeing another. Next, Shelley said she could see the hallway and it had suddenly darkened dramatically. I got up and started to walk around, but when I went into the dining room the light that the others had seen wasn't there, and when I looked back towards the hallway the sense of extreme darkness that Shelley had noticed had gone. The only thing that I really experienced on the ground floor that night was the cold. It felt as if I was running around searching for other people's sensations of the light anomalies and not really seeing them for myself.

'I think I'd really like to go upstairs,' I said.

Mark offered to come with me while Shelley and Bob stayed in the living room.

Mark and I climbed the stairs and decided to spend a little while on the landing itself. We sat on the top steps. I was getting absolutely freezing at this stage, particularly all down my back. I touched Mark's arm – he was like a hot water bottle and said that my hand was like ice.

We decided to move through to Bob and Shelley's room. Immediately I saw an orb of light above the bed on the wall. It was huge. Mark didn't see this as he was behind me and his line of vision was obscured by a lamp-shade. We did both begin to get headaches though. They were pressure headaches which came on slowly.

'Let's try the little girl's bedroom,' I suggested, and we trooped through and waited. I was standing facing the doorway and thought I saw a figure in the hall. It was very solid and my first thought was that it might be a member of the crew. The house was locked down and nobody ought to have been in there, but still, the figure seemed very real. We went out and shone a torch around, but there was no one there. Then we heard a crashing sound from the direction of the stairwell and we ran over. Again, the torches showed nothing.

It was still very chilly and our headaches were getting worse so we decided to go back down and see if Bob and Shelley were all right. Back in the dining room the Stevenses had bundled up under a cover because they were feeling so cold.

'I think you should come and have a look upstairs,' I said to Bob, while Shelley and Mark went out to the Winnebago to monitor us on the screens.

I wished I had brought a big, thick sweater with me. It was absolutely Baltic inside that house. Bob and I climbed the stairs together and we sat on the top steps for a while but saw nothing, so we decided to move on to Bob and Shelley's bedroom. Bob settled down on the bed while I perched on the edge of the mattress.

'Freezing,' I commented, and Bob nodded.

We sat for a few minutes and then we both heard a loud groaning sound from the girl's bedroom across the hallway. I shone a torch through the door and saw that one of the pillows that had been at the head of the bed was halfway down the mattress.

'Anyone been in there?' I asked.

Mark and I had definitely not moved any pillows around when we were up there earlier and Bob and I had not yet been into that room. The crew were all outside. This was a lot of activity for one night.

'Can you hear that?' Bob asked.

There was a low, creaking noise on the stairs.

'Yeah,' I said.

We decided to go down and see what was going on with everyone else. No one had come in from outside so the noises and movements hadn't been caused by any member of the crew. The pillow was on my mind – I wanted to be absolutely sure that, apart from the spirit, Bob and I had definitely been alone up there. I checked with Mark that we definitely hadn't moved any pillows upstairs when we were there before, which he confirmed.

'Right,' I said. 'Let's go back up. Will you come with me this time, Shelley?'

Shelley was rubbing her arms because of the cold.

'Sure,' she said, though I could see she was becoming very frightened.

'We'll be right downstairs,' Mark promised and took Bob off to check some of his ghost-busting equipment to see if the temperature readings had fluctuated or if the movement sensors had been set off.

'If you need to hold my hand, go right ahead,' I offered.

By this time my bones were cold and my ears were aching with the cold. I was becoming obsessed by it, and was fantasizing about wrapping my fingers around a warm cup of tea when I finally went back out to the Winnebago. Shelley and I replaced the pillow and then went into her bedroom. While we were in there we heard a noise in the other bedroom and raced back through. A heart-shaped pillow had appeared in the middle of the other mattress. It had been up at the head of the bed originally. It was impossible that there could be any logical explanation for this.

'I can't wait to hear what Chris has to say about this one,' I said.

Shelley sat on the edge of her daughter's bed.

'Weird,' she said.

No sooner had we settled in the second bedroom than we heard a wailing noise from Shelley's room. We shone a torch over the hallway and one of the pillows that had been carefully placed at the head of the bed was sitting on the mattress further down. I could see that Shelley was spooked badly by this. She was shaking and very nervous.

'Oh my God,' she said.

I found it amazing. This ghost was playing with us. But when I looked at Shelley I realized that she probably couldn't take very much more. It was very disturbing for her.

'Come on,' I replied. 'Perhaps it would be best to go back down. You've been very brave.'

Outside in the Winnebago, Claire had brewed up a big pot of tea. Bob was so cold that his teeth were chattering.

'It's much warmer in your garden than it is in your house!' I teased. 'We should stand out there to warm up.'

Claire fetched some blankets and a coat and Bob and I wrapped ourselves up. Mark was still toasty warm and hadn't been affected by the temperature fluctuations in any way. However, the temperature sensor he had left in the dining room showed a ten-point drop over the course of the evening.

'That's much more than you would expect,' he said. 'And I can't think of a normal reason for it.'

There had been a lot of electrical disturbances on the set that evening all round. The crew had found that some of their battery-operated equipment had shut itself down.

'And my electromagnetic field meter ran out of batteries,' Mark said. 'They were fully charged at the start. That's never ever happened to me before.'

I think all of this had intrigued Chris the sceptic.

'Right,' he said. 'I'm going in to have a look around.'

As ever, I sat watching Chris on the monitor. He sensed nothing as he walked round the darkened house and didn't seem the least bit perturbed by the strange goings on with the pillows upstairs, which he put down to forgetfulness on our part or simply not patting the pillows down properly when we had replaced them so that they tumbled down the length of the bed.

I was beginning to despair of Chris ever accepting that the activities in these houses were not normal. He seemed to be able to come up with endless explanations which he felt ought to be logical, but made no sense when you were actually in the house, with bumps and bangs, moving objects and strange lights. I had never expected him to accept that headaches or chills were actually paranormal, but that night we had had a spirit that was moving objects around while we were on the set. He remained, however, intractable.

Because of all the power failures and difficulties over batteries, the shoot at the Stevenses' house went on very late and it was getting light by the time we had finished, the crew had packed up and Bob and Shelley were left on their own. I was glad that the night was over for them and I thought that Shelley particularly had had a bad time of it. The pillow moving that last time had really shaken her. It was six in the morning by the time we made it back to the hotel. Inside, there were waitresses getting ready for the breakfast shift. I half thought about having some toast and tea before getting into bed but the food at the hotel had been so consistently bad before that I didn't think it was worth it.

'Thank God for bed,' I said to Gemma as I said goodnight to her in the hallway, and I fell down on the mattress and slept until midday.

When I woke up I was still thinking about those pillows moving around.

'That's amazing, isn't it?' I said to Eric.

Eric seemed non-committal.

'I suppose this spirit wants to be helped. She wants to announce her presence.'

It is very rare that a ghost will go that far, though. Very few spirits are able to. I was looking forward to the clearing now. I wanted to meet her.

I got dressed and went downstairs, where I bumped into Mark. We ordered a pot of tea and waited for a while, but no one else seemed to be awake yet. We decided not to brave the hotel food for lunch, so we wandered down the road to a nearby pub where there was a traditional Sunday lunch on the go. Late in the afternoon we came back to the hotel. Erica, a cheery girl who apparently normally worked on *Emmerdale*, had been booked to do my hair and make up. She made a great job of it.

Around five o'clock Claire drove me back to the Stevenses' house and I could feel the excitement and anticipation building in my stomach.

'I think the best place to do the clearing would be in the dining room,' I said, thinking it through and planning things in my head.

I had the impression that Claire was just glad she didn't have to deal with the logistics of anything as difficult as the cellar at Elmtree House. At least this time there wasn't going to be a well in the way!

'Perfect,' she said. 'I have boxes of candles in the boot of the car.'

Gemma had arranged for the pub who had served our

dinner after their kitchen closed the night before to give us a room to use that night so there wouldn't be so many people jammed in the Winnebago. We stayed there most of the evening while the crew set up. Neither Mark nor I were very hungry after our marathon lunch and I only managed a bowl of soup quite late on. It was nice to hang around together and just relax for a few hours, though, and I found that I was really looking forward to doing this clearing.

Back at the house, Claire had made the dining room look beautiful. There was a lovely round table and light-coloured oak chairs and, as always, the place was lit beautifully by a sea of gorgeous candles on every surface. I really liked the way that the candles were different from each other – there were tall ones and tea lights and all shapes and sizes flickering away.

It was only as I entered the dining room that I had any worries. It suddenly struck me that I had to keep my eyes open. This wasn't, after all, a completely standard ghost. I had sensed no epicentre to this haunting and the house completely lacked the usual ominous feeling that hangs around haunted properties.

'What if there isn't a ghost at all?' I suddenly panicked.

No one was prepared to take this seriously – in fact one or two of the crew just laughed.

'You're always all right, Mia,' someone said.

I didn't want to let the cameras down. It's always nerve-racking – not knowing what is actually there or what will happen. There is no rule saying that every spirit wants to tell me their story or give an explanation for why they have been haunting somewhere.

'Well,' I thought to myself, 'I think there is a ghost. And if this time it isn't a big story and there is no song and dance, then that'll just have to be the way that it is.'

I sat down at the table with Shelley and Bob and began to explain that I was going to search their house, find the ghost and do my best to find out why the spirit was here. They both seemed relatively calm – certainly calmer than the night before. I hoped that things were going to go well. Then I took a deep breath, dropped my shoulders and came out of my body to psychically move around the house. I moved off to search the lower floor but didn't see anyone, so I decided to try up above and took the stairs to the bedroom floor. Walking into Bob and Shelley's bedroom I could see immediately that the place looked different from when I had been up there the night before. There was a door that I could see psychically which wasn't there any more – it had been in the original house before the renovations, I thought. The door was open and on the other side, in what looked like a passageway, stood a woman. I stepped backwards to encourage her to come into the room and follow me. She came in and hovered for a moment beside the window, seemingly unwilling to move any further. I reached out to gesture to her and slowly I got her to follow me out into the hallway, downstairs and into the dining area, where she stopped opposite me on the other side of the round table.

She was dressed in an iron-grey blouse with a high neck. There were round, pearl buttons down the front of the blouse, all done up. It was very fitted in style and I had a sense that she had been alive in the 1940s, or perhaps the early 1950s. However, the year 1886 also came into my mind and I still don't really understand why. The woman showed me a coin that had a man's head on it, which made me think that perhaps she did belong to the 1940s after all. In any case, this spirit looked very stressed out. Her face was tense and her eyes were frantic and darting. Her dark hair was pulled back very tightly and she was wearing a flowing skirt.

This was definitely the same spirit that I had seen the day before, but I didn't know why she had changed her outfit. Perhaps, I thought, when I saw her in white beside the fireplace as I had originally walked around, it was only mist generated by her appearance. I hadn't taken a close look at the time because I hadn't wanted to encourage her and I knew that I couldn't switch on fully. Normally, in the case of hauntings, spirits only appear in the clothes that they actually died in. In the case of visitors they might wear anything, or appear in a physical form that is far younger than they were when they had died. Visitors tend to arrive looking as they did in their prime. This woman was no visitor. She did not have the sense of peace and serenity that I always pick up from that kind of spirit. The woman had not passed over when her time had come and was now trapped in the Stevenses' House.

She stood before me, wringing her hands with frustration and anxiety. Pictures began to come into my mind. I saw that the house was back to front, at least it was radically altered from when she lived here. This really distressed the woman. It wasn't only the top part of the house, but the stairs used to be in a different place and she could see the renovations that the Stevens family had made and couldn't understand why her home had changed. On top of this she was terrified, and what scared her most was that she couldn't get out of the house. She ran, full pelt, at the front door and it was as if she bounced off it. That surprised me. Usually ghosts can pass easily through walls, but this woman was trapped in the house. I'd never seen anything like it before and I had an over-whelming feeling of pity for her. It was as if she was being tortured. She had been trapped. She began to grasp her throat and I could see that she couldn't breathe. Then I realized that she had died from smoke inhalation. There had been a fire in the house, but that wasn't what had actu-ally killed her. The smoke had choked her to death first.

'I told them,' she gasped, pointing at Bob and Shelley, when she realized that I understood what she was trying to say.

Then all of a sudden the spirit seemed to recover herself.

'And he's been crying,' she said, pointing again at Bob as if she was telling on him.

The ghost told me that her name was Mary. She was proud of her house and had been happy living there, although her marriage had not been an easy one. Her husband's name was Patrick and he had not been kind to her. When Bob and Shelley first came she didn't like Bob and said she had tried to get rid of him. She had been scared that he would be unkind like her husband, but now she saw he was a good man and was happy for him to stay. In fact, she liked him and had tried to talk to him many times.

The information that Mary was imparting to me was coming over in disconnected fits and starts. She seemed quite distracted, in fact, dodging from one subject to another. Then, out of the blue, she changed tack entirely.

'I couldn't get to the child,' she said.

And I realized that when she had been trapped in the house by the fire a child had died there too. Now the spirit of that child had moved on but the poor woman was tormented that she hadn't been able to reach the child. She had got stuck and couldn't help.

At that point the figure of the ghost suddenly disappeared. I felt panicked. There was something off the wall about this woman. She was erratic and quite strange. I thought that the kind of tortured agony she had suffered at the moment of her death had made her spirit restless and tormented. I also didn't know where on earth she had gone. I came out of my body again and decided to search the house. When I got back upstairs I found her again, right beside the window in Bob and Shelley's room. Looking at her she seemed frustrated almost to the point of lunacy. I have never had a spirit run off like that before. Normally, they are so glad to be able to communicate with someone that it isn't really an option for them to leave abruptly. This woman was totally unpredictable. She was so erratic that it occurred to me she might be very difficult to send over. She might just disappear at any time. But not sending her over was out of the question – I had stirred her up now, and if she didn't pass the haunting would be worse than ever before.

I decided to use my force of will and psychically I called out to her, willing her to come back downstairs into the dining room again. It took a long time. She kept staring back in the direction of the upstairs bedroom and seemed agitated to be away from that room. Once I had her in the dining area again I decided that I had to send her over straight away. I didn't want to give her too much opportunity to disappear, and for me to lose her again.

I called Eric and a doorway opened right behind Mary, but she didn't step into it. In fact, she didn't acknowledge it in any way. It was almost as if she was pulled in, resisting all the way. She moved slowly backwards as if she was being sucked towards the golden light. I said the De Profundis, knowing that this was for her own good. The poor, distracted soul would be far better off on the other side. I knew that there was no reasoning with this woman. There was no point in explaining to her why she ought to allow herself to move into the light. She was mad and distracted and it was best to simply get on with the job.

When she finally went over, the door of light closed behind her and a beautiful, golden snow started to rain down. I watched it, wide eyed. It really is the most beautiful sight. It took me a minute or two to recover myself but when I looked over at Bob and Shelley they were grinning. They could already feel the difference in their home already.

'It's our place now,' Bob said.

Afterwards, we sat around chatting for a while. Bob and I walked around the house and checked every room. It was amazing how much lighter and more pleasant the place felt – like the happy family home it really was. They said that having the ghost in the house had caused problems for them – they had been arguing – but they knew that things were going to get better now. I had that sense myself – the Stevenses were a very close family indeed and I had no doubt that things were going to be good for them.

After we had said goodbye to Bob and Shelley and all the equipment had been removed from their home, we drove back to the hotel. It was two in the morning and I was glad that this would be our last night there. I was so tired that I didn't notice the musty smell around reception any more and once I got to my room I didn't even have enough energy to light a cigarette. I was drained. There was only one more house to go for the series.

'I wonder what they have saved until last,' I thought, as I changed into my nightie and brushed my teeth.

'It looks like I am going to make it, though. I'm not going to collapse or anything,' I smiled to myself. I was really missing home. Being around such a close family had reminded me of my own. I missed chatting to my mother and sitting up for late night cups of tea with my daughter. I missed eating food that I had cooked myself, just opening the fridge and deciding what to have. It would be good to get back after the long round of hotels and restaurant food, endless trains and taxis and lifts in hired cars.

'Just one more,' I thought. 'And fingers crossed the hotel there is better than this one.'

Chapter Seven

The Munday Family's House. Salisbury.
Cleared on 23rd September 2005.

The Mundays have lived in their house for five years. They are ghost hunters and have dabbled with ouija boards. The paranormal phenomena they have experienced in the house include objects moving (books flying off a shelf) and going missing, electrical disturbances, orbs and a number of apparitions including a young child, a monk and a sinister, dark man. The family report highly uncomfortable feelings in some areas of their home which have often been commented upon by visitors.

Evil Enters Like a Needle and Spreads Like an Oak Tree

It was getting to be autumn – in fact the Mundays' house was cleared on the night of the autumn equinox. The weather was changeable the morning I drove up from Kent in my old, cream Rover with my bag on the back seat. One minute it was blazing sunshine – a real Indian summer – and the next it was too cold to have the window down as I zoomed along. It wouldn't be many more weeks before the leaves started turning colour – it's my favourite time of the year, the autumn, when you can kick your way through piles of dead leaves and you can catch that nip in the air sometimes, although it's often still balmy, especially early on in the season.

The week before, as I left Lincolnshire, I'd been told that the last house of the series was in the Salisbury area and I'd decided that I would drive myself over there. It would be good, I thought, to have a car with me this time, rather than needing to get a lift everywhere I went.

Claire had phoned in the morning before I set out to let me know the location of the hotel – just off the main motorway in a service area on the A303. It was about three hours from home.

'Have you got a map?' she had asked.

I had clearly given the impression that my psychic skills didn't extend to navigation and she was worried that I was too haphazard to get myself to the hotel on time.

'Yeah. An AA one,' I laughed. 'Don't worry. I'll be there!'

When I pulled up in the hotel car park and hauled my bag out of the back there was no one from September Films around. In fact, despite the proximity to the nearby motorway, the place seemed deserted. I scanned the car park, but none of the crew cars were parked there and there was no sign of the Winnebago. I thought I'd check in and maybe take a bath – it would be nice to read a book or watch some TV. Just to relax.

'Hello,' I said cheerily to the clerk at the desk, 'I'm booked in for tonight – Mia Dolan. It's a smoking room.'

The clerk smiled and punched in my name on the keyboard in front of her. Then, without really looking at what she was doing, she leant back and picked out a key from the rack on the wall.

'We don't have a smoking room left,' she said, and held out the key towards me.

I must have been tired, I think. Perhaps it was because it was the end of the series, but I got into a paddy. I panicked. This was the closest in my entire life that I have ever come to having a diva fit. Jennifer Lopez may insist on white flowers and mineral water wherever she goes, but I just have to be able to have a cigarette in my room. No question.

'A no smoking room?' I was horrified. 'I can't check in. I won't check in,' I said. 'I have to be able to smoke.'

The clerk shifted nervously on her chair.

'We don't have any smoking rooms,' she said, apologetically. 'They're all taken.'

This would have to happen when there wasn't a cheery production assistant to help me sort it out.

'I can't check in, then,' I said, holding my ground.

'You're with that TV company, aren't you?' the clerk said, and the tone of her voice sounded like an accusation.

I felt ashamed of myself then. I wondered if she thought I was after special treatment because I am on the telly. I'd hate to ever be like that. But telly or no telly I wasn't going to check in if I couldn't light up.

'Can I swap with one of the crew?' I suggested. 'They won't mind. It's just I have to be able to smoke. When I'm working,' I added, to make my nicotine addiction sound somehow more justified.

The girl punched some more digits on the computer and then disappeared into an office at the back of the reception desk. There was nowhere to sit down, so I leant on the counter and waited. It took a while, but when she came out again she had another key in her hand.

'There you go,' she said with a smile.

'Thanks, darling.'

I unpacked in my room and sat on the bed, reading for an hour or two, relishing chain-smoking cigarettes one after the other, and sipping on cups of tea. At about seven there was a knock on the door. When I opened it, Gemma and Claire were in the hallway. The room behind me was obscured by a haze of smoke.

'Blimey, Mia, have you been making kippers in there?' Gemma teased.

We were all hungry by then and decided to drive over to Ainsbury, nearby, to grab some dinner. The shoot wouldn't start until the next day and the rest of the crew either hadn't arrived or were already doing some kind of pre-shoot at the Mundays' house. We drove to The George pub and ordered chicken pies – it was warm and welcoming, a nice traditional bar, and I settled down, telling the girls about my near miss with the no-smoking bedroom. It was pub quiz night at The George and as we were eating, teams were arriving and settling down. By the time our plates were cleared the place was packed.

'Looks like fun,' Claire said.

The quizmaster was handing out sheets of paper at a table at one end of the room and the teams were assembling, milling round, buying rounds of drinks and setting out chairs around their team tables.

'Shall we enter?' Gemma asked. 'Just for the laugh?'

It was still quite early and it was nice to be somewhere so lively.

'Let's give it a go,' I said. 'Why not?'

I never knew that people took pub quizzes quite so seriously. On closer examination we discovered that many of the teams were made up of experts in different subjects and from the snippets of conversation we overheard we could tell that some of them entered more than one quiz a week. As the quizmaster quietened everyone down and the questions started, the atmosphere became hushed and competitive. It wasn't long before Claire, Gemma and I realized that we were rubbish! We didn't have a sports expert on our team, for a start. In fact, we didn't have anyone who was any good at history either. We got worse and worse as we became more demoralized. At the end of each round the quizmaster read out the results and our performance every time was lamentable. I am glad that we didn't come last – but it was a close thing and we were only a few points off it.

It was midnight by the time we rolled home to bed at the hotel. I changed into my nightdress and decided to have a final cup of tea and a cigarette before I settled down. I switched out the lights and from the window I could see car headlamps in the middle distance, roaring along the nearby motorway. It looked pretty – like a random pattern against the night sky. I felt glad that for this series at least, the Mundays' house was the last one I was coming to for a while. It had been a long run of intense work and I could do with a break.

'I hope this house is a good one,' I said out loud, hardly thinking.

'Watch yourself here. Be careful.' Eric's voice came back at me.

He made me start. Eric often pops up like that, in the dark, out of nowhere.

'You gave me a fright, Eric. What do you mean?' I asked.

'Watch yourself. Be careful,' he repeated. 'This one isn't going to be easy.'

'Right,' I said. 'OK then.' I sipped the last of my tea and thought it was probably best to get a good night's sleep.

In the morning it was cold. The crew traipsed down for breakfast late and at midday I drove to a different hotel where the psychometry test had been set up. It was the usual case – a far smarter room than the ones we were actually staying in, with everything laid out on a table and a comfortable chair for me to sit on. This time on the table there was a plain gold ring, a pendant, a pocket watch, a digital watch, a carved cork box, a black leather belt and a plectrum.

I paused before picking up any of the items. They didn't look old enough, in the main, for me to be able to sense strong feelings. Often items have to be older and very treasured for the feelings to be clear and strong and this collection looked dubious in that respect. I decided to start with the ring, which at least looked old. The feeling I got from it when I placed it on my palm was that it wasn't a wedding ring, even though it looked like one. This had been worn on the pinkie finger, and had belonged to two people, passed down from one generation to another.

Next I came to the pendant. It wasn't an old item and was mounted on a leather string. However, the minute I touched it my heart started racing and I felt panicky. Eric's voice boomed in my ear, 'See what I mean? Be careful, Mia.' Something was wrong in the house if I was picking up this kind of feeling already. The pendant must have been worn a lot to be so strongly ingrained with the sensation of the wearer. I saw the word 'sweetheart' and felt that there had been two of these pendants, a matching set.

After that I turned to the watches, but didn't get anything very conclusive from either of them. When I held the digital watch I saw pictures of a kitchen and of the watch falling off a wrist, but there was nothing strong about the images.

The carved box gave more details. I could hear alarm bells ringing in my head. I saw flames and thought there had been cards kept inside the box, and that it had been placed in a living room on a sideboard. Again, none of the feelings were particularly strong.

The belt belonged to a level-headed man. He was fearless, though, almost to the point of being foolish. It came into my head that he would get on with Mark from Ghost UK. I also saw that this man had been arguing over some trouble and that rather than arguing, it would have been better to stick together over whatever was causing the problem.

Last of all, the plectrum surprised me. I expected the image of a guitar to arrive when I picked it up but there was none. When I tried to imagine a guitar it dissolved in my mind's eye, the strings breaking. This plectrum hadn't been used to play music. I moved it around flat on the table in front of me, and it came to me that that was what it was for – pointing to things. As if it had been used on a ouija board.

'Oh no,' I thought. I could see what Eric meant. The images and the feelings I was getting from these items were worse than any of the other houses we'd been to. There was a sense of badness – a place that had been tainted. I could see a nice, family home. Somewhere comfortable and relaxed with all the chaos and clutter of family life. But then there was something very deeply wrong. I had a sense that this wasn't a house with a regular haunting. This spirit had been encouraged to come – someone in the house had invited it.

'Eric is right,' I thought. 'This one is going to be tough.'

Instead of just waiting as the crew dismantled the room, I took a bottle of water from the mini bar and went outside. I sipped the cold liquid, walking up and down the tarmac of the car park as I ran through what I had just seen and felt.

'They had to save the best till last, I guess,' I thought. Though of course, the crew might not have known that in this house I could already sense something particularly ominous. I was taking tiny sips, wondering what it would be like inside the haunted house if just picking up that pendant had made my heart race. It certainly wasn't a good sign.

'Well, I'm here now,' I thought. 'And if I don't do it no one else will.'

The crew began to come out with their cameras packed away.

'Come on, Mia,' Gemma said cheerily.

I didn't feel cheery at all, but I got back into the car and followed the crew to the location.

It is, as always, on approaching the house that my memory becomes vivid. All psychic experience is vivid, really. It's one of the markers that what is happening is psychic. I am often annoyingly unaware of the 'real' world. I can't remember the colour of the paint in my own hallway, but I can recall in vibrant detail psychic dreams or the way I feel when I send over a spirit.

I was standing on the street. They had done my make up and checked the cameras and I walked into a cul-de-sac to approach the house on my own. It surprised me, given the strength of the psychometry, that I didn't feel much as I was looking at the house from the outside. It was a normal, family home – a semi-detached building on the right side of a dead-end street. I put my hand on the door handle and entered the front door at the side of the house, going inside and standing in the hallway with the stairs to my right. Immediately I felt nauseous. There was a worried, sick feeling in the pit of my stomach and I was anxious.

'This isn't very good,' I said as I walked into the living room, and knew immediately that people had been scared in this room. There had been noises and electrical disturbances. This came to me as an intuition.

I moved on to the kitchen. It was a cheerful, brightly painted room but I had an image of a family running out of the back door in fright. I felt horribly uneasy, as if something was looming over me. I didn't like this house at all.

As I climbed the stairs the feeling got heavier. There was a room with a bunk bed that belonged to the girls in this family.

'I wouldn't like to have to sleep in here,' I said.

The atmosphere felt heavy and the sick feeling in my stomach was getting worse. The house was having a very strong, physical effect on me. I took a few deep breaths to try to control the nausea. Then I pressed on. The place felt all wrong – the whole house seemed to be affected and so far there was no sense of an epicentre to the haunting. Things were not right.

In the adults' double bedroom I had the sensation that someone had peered into the room from the hallway and that the bed had trembled.

Worst of all, moving on to the boys' room, I knew that things had been seen there. Something had been trying to interact with the children in this house. I didn't want to say anything on film because I am always very careful where children are involved, but this being, this ghost, if it was one, wanted to hurt the children who lived here. I didn't feel angry or defensive – I was too sickly for that. Mostly I simply felt worried.

My own view was that this wasn't a human spirit. I was not dealing with a 'normal' haunting – a grumpy, bad-tempered ghost who hadn't crossed over. There was no epicentre to what had been going on and the feelings were too negative and too strong. In truth I didn't know exactly what was here. I felt confused, sick and disoriented. I would have to be careful in this house, which was in the grip of something very bad; something that wasn't human. I had a strong sense of Evil here, like in the flat in Sheerness years ago or the pet supplies warehouse I cleared. I didn't feel panicky – only very sick and heavily weighed upon.

I decided to go outside before meeting the family. I needed a minute or two to gather my thoughts and regain control of my wild heart rate and nauseated stomach. Claire fetched me some water to sip and when someone offered me a chocolate biscuit I almost retched. I consciously had to calm myself down and breathe deeply. People often think of being psychic as something that is very much removed from the physical world, but in this house there was something so wrong that it was affecting me very strongly all through my body. I made a conscious decision that I had to be selfish here. I had to look after myself more than I normally would have done. I had to save my strength.

Once I had recovered I went back into the house to meet the family. On entering I felt unwell, but this time I didn't open up psychically. I was able to control my feelings so that instead of the panicked sickness when I walked round earlier, I only felt slightly under the weather.

Nicola and Mel Munday were a lovely young couple. This was Nic's second marriage and she had five children. She was a lively, vibrant woman with dark hair and eyes. Mel was a big bloke – a binman – and I couldn't imagine him being frightened of anything. They had a nice feeling of unity about the two of them and seemed very well matched.

Nic and Mel were different from any of the other *Haunted Homes* families in that they were well versed in the phenomena of the psychic world. Both had been fascinated by the paranormal for years and regularly investigated hauntings and other paranormal activity. Nic organized a paranormal research group on the web. Although they were both scared of what was happening in their house, they didn't seem as completely 'freaked' as any of the other families I had met over the course of the series. In a way, I thought, it was better that way; better that this kind of thing should have been happening in their house. After all, it wasn't a human spirit here. Perhaps these people were better equipped to understand and deal with that.

I started by going through the psychometry – the ring that wasn't a wedding ring belonged to Nic's granny and she used to wear it on her little finger just as I saw. One by one I went through the other items and the only thing that made no sense to them was the fire image that I had picked up from the carved cork box. Then, when I got to the plectrum the couple admitted that it had never been used for guitar playing and that they had been doing ouija boards. They said that they used the ouija whenever their paranormal investigation group went to haunted places.

'Bloody hell,' I said, wide-eyed. 'That is so dangerous.'

I explained why ouija boards are so bad – how you can't tell what you will get when you issue an invitation into the spirit world, and how I had had experience before with evil entities bent on causing misery. I explained that they hold on hard to the world and are difficult to get rid of.

'That's what I think you might have,' I concluded.

Nic and Mel were worried and both felt guilty about the effect the haunting was having on the children. I didn't blame them. The entity had definitely been targeting the kids, who were all sleeping together in one bedroom because they didn't like being split up at night.

I told Nic and Mel about the activity that I had picked up in the house when I first walked through and they confirmed there had been bizarre electrical activity. At one time, just sitting in the kitchen in the daylight, an orb had passed between them. Both Nic and Mel had seen apparitions, including a little girl (this apparition appeared not only to Mel but to one of the children), a monk and a very large man swathed in black.

'Things go missing around the house all the time,' Nic

told me. 'You'll look for ages and then whatever it is will suddenly appear on top of a work surface you know you have checked earlier. Once my credit card went missing, I looked everywhere and then it turned up on top of my handbag, steaming hot in the centre. It was so hot I could hardly touch it.'

Mel said, 'I've often felt sick. I'm not surprised you feel that too.'

Most of all, the couple were sure that whatever was in their house was feeding off negative energy.

'There is a form of manipulation going on with the thing,' Nic said.

This didn't surprise me. An evil entity will try to provoke fear and unhappiness – these emotions make it stronger.

'I can feel a buzz, like an electric tingling,' Mel explained, 'like the anticipation of what it is going to do.'

Through the ouija board, Nic and Mel had been interacting regularly with five different figures. Now this in itself was a sign that something was very wrong. I have never been in a house with more than one or two ghosts (that is to say, not visitors, but actual hauntings). I suppose in the case of an ancient, ancient house more than one person might be left behind, but the idea of five hauntings all at once just didn't wash with me. If anything it confirmed that there was one evil entity in this house – one dreadful, evil presence that had been invited in and let loose, that was taking on different forms for its own amusement. It was playing with the family, getting stronger all the time.

'It's lying to you,' I said. 'It'll take on different voices. It'll mess with your head. It'll appear as a child – people are a lot less likely to get rid of the ghost of a child. Next time it'll come as something scary-looking and dark. It is playing with you. What you have here is an entity. Nothing you've seen is human. It is very, very dark.'

The couple were shocked. They knew that there had to be something heavy haunting them, but the idea that it was actually evil, and not in any way human, was sinking in slowly.

'It's been like this for about a year,' Nic said, shocked. 'Oh my God.'

As Mark and Chris went around the house trying to explain the strange activity, I went to have a lie down in the Winnebago. I felt nervous and completely drained and I needed some time away from the others.

'Eric,' I called out.

And Eric appeared next to me.

'This could all go belly up, you know,' I said.

'Be careful,' Eric repeated himself.

'No joke. It's strong, isn't it?'

'You can do it. The power of good is always stronger,' Eric comforted me.

I closed my eyes and tried to relax. I had a bad feeling in the pit of my stomach and even though I was out of the house for the moment, I was worried. This entity had been around for a year. It was strong and clever and had been feeding off the family's distress. I tried to make myself angry on their behalf but all I could summon up was my own determination to take care and make sure that no one got hurt. There were a lot of people around for the evil to play with.

I heard Chris on camera saying that he didn't think there was anything inexplicable going on, even if some of what was being reported by the family was a bit odd. For one moment I felt envious of him – I would have far preferred not to be able to feel this entity. Lucky sceptics.

'Just focus,' I told myself, 'and sort it out.'

The crew set up for the vigil and the rest of us went out to eat. I didn't feel much like food, but I managed to eat something. I was a lot quieter than usual and a couple of people asked me if I was all right. 'Fine,' I said. It was true. I was all right, I was just saving myself. This vigil was going to be difficult – I had to stay shut down psychically and I was not relishing the thought of spending hours overnight in the house. Just a few minutes during the day had made me feel dreadful.

We returned to the house after the meal and decided to set up in the kitchen to start with. There wasn't an epicentre to this haunting but the kitchen was a good place to get going as it was where Nic and Mel used the ouija board. I knew I had to pace myself and keep shut down, no matter what. If I opened up the entity would be called to me and as I didn't want to take it on and clear the house that night, the best idea was to lay low.

Three – two – one and the lights went out. Mark, Nic, Mel and I were all sitting around the kitchen table. It didn't take long after my eyes became accustomed to the darkness before I saw a large, black shape, like a piece of furniture, beside Mel. I thought that perhaps I had lost my bearings and there was some furniture there, so I asked Mel. He put out his hand and it passed straight through the shape. It definitely wasn't solid. Then Mel said he could see a shadow behind me too – just a couple of feet away at my back. I was getting the creeps – this reminded me of that prowling, dark hunter in the flat in Sheerness. Something was in the kitchen with us. Something dark. It was prowling around as we sat at the table. I could feel a sensation of cold on my back – not a slight breeze but a freezing block of ice, solid and almost painful. It was intense, right between my shoulder blades.

I said, 'I can feel it. It's against my shoulders.'

Then there was a creaking from upstairs. It was as if someone was walking across the hallway, although we all knew the house had been completely emptied and we were alone.

We decided to press on and move around the house to see if there was anything to come across other than the creaking. Mark and Nic went into the living room while I went upstairs with Mel who strode confidently up the stairs ahead of me. It was unusual for the families to be so self-assured and it was nice not to have to comfort the Mundays. Mel and Nic were used to hauntings and they wanted to investigate. While we were all slightly on edge, I have to say that the atmosphere was less nervy than usual. Mel and Nic had done this kind of thing before.

Upstairs it felt cold. The ball of ice was still pressing against my back. It was so uncomfortable that I was squirming, trying to relieve the feeling. But I couldn't get rid of it. I was not well. A headache started pounding, right in the middle of my forehead, and I felt sick.

Mel was suffering too, though to a lesser degree. He felt something touch his arm as if it was brushing past him. We waited a while but nothing else happened.

'Let's go back downstairs,' I said.

When we got there I decided to try going back upstairs with Nic, leaving the boys in the living room. Nic and I climbed the stairs and sat on the top step. I didn't want to open up, even though the cold feeling on my back was really hurting now and I knew that if I did reveal myself psychically I would probably come to understand why I was feeling that way. I was frustrated that I didn't know what was really going on – I was suffering from the symptoms of this haunting, but couldn't see the causes. Even without my psychic sense I knew that what was in this house was a very heavy, dangerous entity. Warning bells were ringing in my ears. In every other house in the series the vigil had been interesting. It had been good to feel what it was like to experience a haunting without the psychic sense. I might have had headaches or felt cold but that was only sensation. Here there was danger. It was different. Here I didn't like it at all. I felt exposed and ill.

Nic went into one of the bedrooms and when she was in there she felt a touch on her arm, just as Mel had earlier.

'I'm going to stay in here,' she said, 'and see if it happens again.'

I decided to go back downstairs to talk to Mel. I wondered if he had been touched on the same side and if this had ever happened to either of them before. Also, by this stage I was feeling pretty rough. When I descended into the hallway I realized that the rooms downstairs were empty. Mel and Mark had abandoned the vigil and gone out to the Winnebago. I decided to wait for Nic, who was still at the top of the building, but I wanted to sit down. The atmosphere was draining me. I hauled myself through to the kitchen and sat back down at the table. I started to relax, thinking, 'Well at least we won't be in here much longer.' I was looking forward to sitting down in the Winnebago and recovering. Then out of the blue I felt a sharp poke on my shoulder blade. It wasn't only a brush against my skin, it was as if I had been deliberately hurt, jabbed by something hard. It was sore. I jumped up, squawking with the discomfort and the fright. It was the last thing I was expecting. There was nothing behind me, of course. Nothing I could see. It was clear, though, even without my psychic sense switched on, that there was a being here in the kitchen with me. It was malevolent. It was trying to hurt me. I sank back down in my seat, thinking that when Nic came down we would go outside. And immediately I felt the pain again – a sharp poke right in between my shoulder blades.

'Right,' I said out loud, knowing the crew were monitoring me on the screens. 'It's done it again. Come in here and see what you can pick up on the thermal cameras.'

The crew came in. I think watching us this time had been pretty scary for them. The atmosphere was charged. I knew I probably looked pretty rough. Also, during the course of filming the rest of the series I had taken anything that happened in my stride, and the haunting in this house was obviously really affecting me. It must have been a bit like your heart surgeon looking worried. Everyone was taking things seriously.

At last Nic came downstairs and I decided to leave the crew to it. They didn't seem to be able to find anything on the special cameras. I had had enough.

Out in the Winnebago I slumped down in one of the comfortable chairs.

'Blimey,' I said, 'this is tough.'

My back was cold and aching from where I had been poked and I felt sick.

Mel was game, though. He decided to go back in alone and see what happened, so out came the crew and we sat around to watch Mel on the monitor at the front of the caravan. For a few moments I thought that I was going to be fine, but suddenly a wave of extreme sickness came over me and I had to run outside to vomit. As I was making my way through the door one of the crew said, 'Mia, can we film you?'

'No!' I shouted.

That's the last thing I wanted on TV. Pictures of me, vomiting from spirit activity.

Mark followed me out with a cup of water. I still felt ill, but I was getting better, although I was absolutely freezing. I was still retching intermittently.

'I've read somewhere,' Mark said, 'that evil entities that want to possess you get in via the shoulder blades.'

'Cheers,' I said.

Personally, I try not to read up too much. I avoid those books. I don't want anything giving me ideas and I'd rather feel my own way around problems, trusting my senses.

Right now, though, my instinct was just to get away. Beside Mark, Eric appeared.

'Keep shut down and you'll be all right,' he said.

As we climbed back into the Winnebago the crew told us that Mel thought he had seen something inside the house. I had had enough. Outside a thick, autumn fog had descended and it was cold. I could feel myself shaking. Physically, this had simply been too much. It was very late now and time to finish.

We went back into the house one last time.

'I'll be glad to get out of this house tonight,' I said as Mark, Nic and Mel sat around the kitchen table. The Mundays' house had affected me more than any other, but the crew said that it was the one where they had picked up the least activity on their technical equipment. For myself, I reckoned it was half past four in the morning and I didn't need proof of anything. My back was still cold and painful and I knew that whatever was in the Mundays' house would be waiting for me the next day.

'Can someone take me back to the hotel?' I asked.

I was feeling better now, bit by bit, but I knew it was time to go.

One of the production assistants drove my car because I was not capable of doing it myself. It took twice as long as it should have because the visibility was so low – the fog was getting thicker and thicker.

I sank into my bed and closed my eyes. I was too washed out to even light up a cigarette.

'Could have been a no smoking room after all,' I mumbled to myself, and I fell into the deep sleep that I definitely needed.

Six hours later I woke up still feeling tired. I sat up in bed with a cup of tea and realized that for the first time

I didn't have any performance anxiety about the clearing. This wasn't a ghost I wanted to get details from. I was not interested in answering the family's questions or making a good show for the cameras. I'd try all that but I was simply keyed up to sort this one out. That was all that mattered.

I got washed and dressed and joined everyone in the hotel lobby for something to eat. I decided that I had to explain to the crew what was going on. Although I had been explicit with the family, not everyone would have heard me telling them.

'This isn't a regular spirit,' I told the assembled table. 'We have a demonic haunting in this house.'

One or two of the crew looked blankly back at me. One girl's eyes zoomed towards the floor.

'I want you to know that when I start this clearing, whatever happens I won't stop. But this is going to be difficult. And it is more dangerous than anything else we have dealt with in the series before. Please, keep your eyes open and be careful,' I said.

Although I was still tired I felt completely focused. I was getting angry – how dare this thing feed on the Mundays' fear? How dare this thing try to hurt me?

After everyone had finished eating we got into the cars and drove over to the Mundays' house. The director interviewed the family, talking about their reactions to the night before. Off camera Mel told me that he felt angry about the clearing.

'Me too,' I said. 'I feel angry that this entity is here at all.'

'No,' he explained, 'it doesn't make any sense. I feel angry that you are going to clear it. As if I want it to stay!'

I felt worried at that. Mel was a big bloke and I hoped that the entity wasn't going to try to use him to somehow stop its expulsion. Evil has no conscience. It'll do whatever it can. I explained to Mel that he might be finding himself influenced by the entity; that he had to be strong.

'It's confusing,' he said, 'to find myself wanting something I know I don't want at all.'

Mel told me that the last time he did the ouija board the entity had spelled out 'You can't get rid of me.'

'It's lying,' I said. 'I am going to shift it.'

We set up the clearing in the kitchen with candles everywhere. It was the autumn equinox and the crew were all chatting about how much extra atmosphere that gave this episode of the series. I was not so affected by the date – I gave my normal talk for the camera about what I was going to do, though I noticed that instead of saying, 'I am going to search the house,' I said, 'I am going to try to search the house.' Instead of saying, 'I am going to clear this spirit,' I said, 'I am going to try to clear this spirit.' I was definitely nervous.

'Keep a handle on your emotions,' I told everyone, although I was thinking of Mel, because he had already worried me with his confession that he didn't want me to clear his home. 'It might make you feel angry so fight how you feel.'

I took a couple of deep breaths. The house was absolutely silent and I knew that everyone was on edge. I entered The Zone and as I did so I left my body. I travelled up the stairs. There was nothing in the boys' room. Next I went to Mel and Nic's bedroom. In there I saw a man. He was tall – about six feet three inches – with mid-length, dark hair. He was wearing a faded red waist-coat, a collarless grey shirt and baggy dark trousers. In this form, the entity was sitting on the bed, confident, with his hands behind his head. He was sneering at me.

'There you are,' I said. 'Come on. Come downstairs.'

He swung his legs and got up over the side of the bed, grinning unpleasantly. Then he leaned against the wall with his arms crossed.

'If there weren't TV cameras downstairs,' I thought, 'I would start the clearing here.' But I had to get him back into the kitchen where everyone else was waiting. I backed away, thinking that he'd follow. I knew I wanted to stay ahead of him. I didn't want him to touch me, especially now I was in an out-of-body state. Alarm bells were ringing in my mind about that. It was only an instinct, but I knew I didn't want him to lay his hand on me, no matter what.

Gradually, as I backed off, he followed me slowly out into the hall and down the stairs. I didn't take my eyes off him for a moment. As we came into the kitchen he leaned heavily against the fridge freezer with his arms crossed, as if he was saying, 'Right then, what are you going to do? Go on, try it.'

I asked him to talk to me to see if I could get some kind of story from him for the cameras.

Immediately images came into my mind. There were some stone steps that led down into a cellar and then a separate image of a big room with dark furniture and uneven ground outside. I asked him where he was from and I got the name of a place called Manthed Barnham, which seemed odd. Then he said the name Mark.

He laughed at me, as if he was taking the mickey. This was a parody of a clearing, I realized. He was making himself seem like a normal spirit, something human. But he wasn't.

Then the entity started saying awful things about Mel and Nic. He was taunting them. I didn't pass on any of the horrible comments, sexual slurs or swearing that were pouring from his lips. He walked across and clapped his hands right next to Mel's face as if to say, 'Who's brave now?' or 'You can't see me, can you?'

'Invitation only,' he sneered.

And then by intuition it came to me. I knew that he hadn't been called up in this house. He had come from another location where Mel and Nic had been ghost hunting. He had followed them home.

'Can't get back,' he said, which I took to mean that he couldn't return to the place where he had been called up, but was stuck at the Mundays' house, where he had been enjoying tormenting the family. His whole presence was malevolent and challenging and I didn't feel I could trust anything the spirit was telling me. Sometimes when I speak to a ghost I have a sense of completion – that they are telling me their story, getting it off their chest before they leave. This felt extremely unsatisfactory and I was beginning to get sick and feel cold. 'Enough is enough,' I reckoned, and I decided it was time to send him over.

Eric appeared beside me, and it came into my mind that I didn't want the door to appear next to me. But then, oddly, no door appeared at all. Instead, a tube of golden light came down from above. In about ten seconds it engulfed the entity and he completely disappeared.

There had been no struggle.

I said the De Profundis with real conviction and suddenly felt a massive sense of relief. As I came out of my trance-like state I looked around the room.

Mel and Nic were happy. I took them aside and told them some of the slurs the spirit had been spouting at them. I thought it was best that once we were off camera they should know what he had said. They told me that the entity had actually been extremely rude about their sex life before – when they did the ouija board first of all. The crew started blowing out candles but something was still on my mind, and although everyone else seemed happy, I was unsettled. It had been too easy. I knew no one else could see that. Probably, from the outside, this clearing looked like any other. But given the intensity of the spirit there hadn't been enough of a struggle. When I remembered battling down the spirit in the pet supplies warehouse, by comparison this had been a piece of cake.

We all had a cup of tea and Mel and Nic chatted away as the crew dismantled the equipment. I gave them my mobile number, just in case. I had a feeling, a bad feeling, that it wouldn't be long before they were in touch. There was something here that I couldn't put my finger on. But when I reached out psychically there was nothing in the house for me to worry about. It didn't stop the doubts in my mind – I just didn't know what to do about them.

At about two in the morning I drove back to the hotel. In my room I called for Eric.

'What's wrong with this?' I asked him. I couldn't get a handle on what had gone on but I knew something that wasn't right.

'It lies,' Eric said simply.

'And is it a human spirit? Is it a human spirit so bad that it is beyond redemption?'

'Yes,' Eric said, sadly. 'But he has lied to you. It is evil now. Not human any more. And it lies.'

One of the annoying things about talking to Eric is that he doesn't tell me information that I don't solicit. I have to learn by my own failures. I have to work things out for myself. It's always been like that for me. That night I thought Eric was saying to me that the spirit had lied – his name wasn't Mark and he didn't come from Manthed Barnam. I should have listened more to my own intuition and pushed for a clearer explanation. As it was I went to bed, I didn't sleep a wink, and the next morning I left for London.

Two days later I was in West Kensington. I was meeting a journalist for an interview in a pub on the North End Road, when I got a call from Mel. He was in a panic.

'It's the same stuff,' he said. 'We've heard banging. We've had footsteps on the landing. The whole house has a horrible stink in it, like sulphur. Our eldest girl had a friend over and they were in the front room when the hoover started shaking. We tried to tell the girls that it wasn't important – that it was a new hoover and that the balance must have gone on it. But it was shaking violently, Mia. The kids didn't buy our explanation. What can we do?'

I couldn't leave the family like that. And I suppose I had known deep down that I was going to get a call from them, because I hadn't been satisfied myself the night of the clearing.

'I'll come straight away,' I said. 'I'll be there tonight.'

'Thanks,' said Mel. 'I don't think we can handle this much longer.'

I finished the interview and then I phoned September Films, who agreed to send a single cameraperson called Rachel to document what was going on. I was to meet her at the station in Salisbury that evening. So I got in my car and drove out of town.

Rachel arrived at Salisbury station and I was there to meet her. She was a pretty brunette, absolutely laden down with equipment. I had seen her before at one of the other houses and I supposed this was a big break for her. She had sound recording equipment to set up as well as the camera.

'This is no frills,' I said. I wasn't in the mood for playing to a camera. It was too serious for that. 'We just have to get rid of this thing. So just get the camera rolling and we'll get on with it.'

It was nine at night by the time we got to the Mundays' house. Rachel went in to interview them about what had been going on in my absence before I went in to see what I could do. I sat in the car feeling terrible. I had let everyone down. I thought back to my conversation in the hotel room with Eric. When he said, 'It lies,' he meant that it had lied about going over. It was just like Eric to hold back from laying the explanation on a plate for me. I know I have to experience things myself in order to learn. It's always been that way for me. This entity had faked its own crossing in order to get me out of the house. Now I was furious. How dare it!

I sat going over things in my mind until Rachel opened the front door and motioned for me to come in. Mel and

Nic had sent the kids over to a friend's house so we were adults only, thank goodness. As soon as I walked through the front door I was bowled over by the sulphurous stink. The house reeked of it and I was not picking it up psychically. Everyone could smell it. Rachel felt sick. When I opened up psychically I could feel the same, terrible atmosphere as I had on the night of the Mundays' vigil. The entity was clearly still in residence.

'I'm sorry this has happened,' I said. 'I made a mistake. I misjudged the situation. It's my fault.'

I walked right round the house to check every room. There was nothing specific to pick up, only the heavy, dull feeling of something being very wrong. I came back down into the living room.

'Where is your ouija board? Did you get rid of it?' I asked.

'It's in the kitchen,' Nic said. 'We didn't use it again.'

'Right. First things first. I'll take it away,' I said.

Nic looked shocked.

'But can't we hold onto it?' she asked. 'We won't use it or anything.'

'If you don't want to use it, what's the problem? I think it's best to get everything connected to this entity out of the house. I'll take it away with me,' I insisted.

'It's strange,' said Nic. 'I don't want it to go.'

We sat down to have a chat about that. I felt that it was the same thing that had happened before when Mel didn't want me to do the clearing. Nic didn't understand her feelings – she recognized that they didn't make any sense.

'Look,' I said, laying the board on the table, 'I'm not clearing anything until that board is out of the house.'

'You're not going to like this,' Mel admitted. 'But Mia, there are two boards.'

'Both of them, then,' I said. 'Definitely.'

One of the boards was completely unused, but I felt that in this situation neither could stay in the house. Nic handed them over and I put the boards in the boot of my car, out of harm's way.

Back in the house I asked to be left alone in the kitchen for a while. I wanted to ask Eric a couple of questions. I was beginning to feel enormous fury building up inside me. What an imposition this entity was! I was not going to hang about – I was itching to deal with it and clear the house properly, but still I thought it was best to make sure that I was going ahead in the right way.

'Eric,' I called out and, as ever, Eric appeared.

'What did I do wrong?' I asked, deciding not to ask Eric the other question in my mind – 'Why didn't you tell me?'

'You have to revoke the invitation,' he said. 'It came by invitation. It's the only way it is allowed to come. And you have to revoke that. And I didn't tell you before because you need to experience these things. You have to find out for yourself.'

I ignored this information because in my mind a chant was forming:

You're not wanted.
You're not entitled.
You're not invited.
The invitation is revoked.
You cannot break the first rule.

The first rule is that an entity can only come by invitation.

'Thanks, Eric,' I said. 'I should have followed my instincts. I knew there was something wrong.'

I glanced up and noticed that it might not be the autumn equinox but this time it was perfect timing. The clock in the kitchen was standing at a minute to midnight. We hadn't planned this, it had just panned out exactly right. I went back into the living room.

'I'm ready to do the clearing now,' I said. 'I'm not going to try to talk to it. I'm not going to do anything for the camera. No frills. I am just going to clear this house.'

Rachel jumped to the camera and set it rolling. There were no candles, only one electric bulb. Mel and Nic were in no particular position. I stood in the middle of the room and opened up.

I didn't want to call the entity to me. I knew I couldn't trust it and I didn't want to fall for any of its tricks again. I was going to clear the whole house – a saturation clearing, not aimed at a specific entity, but spread like a blanket over the whole of the affected area.

I said the chant three times as I psychically rose high in the air, seeing the house from above as if it was laid out in the form of a plan. I concentrated hard on maintaining my belief that I had a complete right to be there. I had no qualms, only the absolute authority that good would prevail. I held on to that belief as I chanted and from above I could see a golden light glowing in every room. I said the De Profundis and then, immediately, everything changed. The house seemed clearer and brighter and the entity was gone. The smell had disappeared. As I came out of the psychic state I realized that I was rocking on my feet, deep in concentration. The place felt different, I realized.

'I think it's gone,' I said.

Mel set off to walk around the house to check it. When he came back he had his arms outstretched and he was crying. He gave me a big hug.

'Thank you,' he said. 'It is gone.'

I apologized again. This was what I should have done in the first place and I felt like an idiot for being fooled. Mel and Nic were just happy; they could feel the incredible difference in their home. I wished them all the best.

'Good luck,' I said, as Rachel gathered up her equipment. We decided to check into the hotel for the night, rather than driving so late.

I felt elated. I felt that I had done it properly this time. I suppose there is always more to learn, but this had been a harsh lesson. When I got to the hotel, for the first time since leaving the Mundays' house a few days before, I slept deeply and well.

The next morning Rachel got the train back to London and I was all set to drive home. When I got out to the car though, I had a shock. The car had been quite neat and tidy when I parked it the night before. Now the doors were still locked, but everything in the back had been thrown, torn, moved about. There were cigarette stubs on the floor. Water had been poured everywhere from a plastic bottle that I was sure I had left on the front seat. Papers and maps were strewn around. I laid my hand on the boot as I looked at it all, realizing the ouija boards were still stowed away in there, out of sight.

'If you think that's going to bother me, forget it!' I said.

I burned the boards on neutral ground (where no one lives) a few days later. And I went back to Kent with the intention of putting my feet up for quite a while. There was clearly bad energy still hanging about.

Epilogue

like my brother, Peter, who visit from time to time and give me advice. Perhaps that is what those other people are counting. I only have to think about Eric and he's there for me, which is different from any of the other spirits I have seen, who each come in their own time, whenever they want to.

As far as I know Eric only appears to me. No one else can see or hear him. That isn't the same with Pete, for example, because some years ago he appeared to my mother in a dream. This phenomenon is not that unusual. Often, this occurs when people are asleep (and at their most relaxed), and I am often asked what the difference is between this kind of visitation (a spirit coming to see you) and a dream. How can you tell if it is only your subconscious mind working or whether something paranormal has happened? My answer to that is that in a paranormal experience the world is still real. That is to say, if it is a full moon outside, it will be a full moon in your experience. If it's a Tuesday, it will still be a Tuesday. You know the person who is visiting you is dead, and you know that you are asleep. And in a visitation you will feel calm – not upset in any way. The detail will be vivid – more than in any ordinary dream. Your recall will be exact. When it happens, you know it's extraordinary, you just have to trust it.

When Pete came to see Mum she woke up in the middle of the night. The moon was very, very bright and cast shadows all over the house, through the windows. Mum got up in her nightie and walked through to what had been Pete's room. There he was, sitting on the edge of the bed. He was wearing a pair of baggy trousers but didn't have any top on. She could see his body, exactly as it had been in life, very clearly because of the moonlight. He had a tattoo on his arm – a rotten, cheap tattoo of a snake he'd had done that I always thought looked dreadful.

'Are you all right?' she asked him.

'I'm fine,' said Pete. 'I've come to put your mind at rest, Mum. Things are going to be good for our family.'

He told her that I was going to do well. That Angela, his girlfriend would be OK, although she would have a rocky road to navigate. That Francesca his daughter would be with me (all of which subsequently happened). And that Mum shouldn't worry. Everything was as it should be. Mum sat on the bed next to him and stroked his arm. She has a vivid memory of her fingers running over his tattoo.

After a while chatting Pete said, 'I have to go now,' and said goodbye. Mum hugged him and she told me later that she could feel he had a real, solid body. And then he was gone.

When she woke up again Mum was in bed. At that time my father was still alive.

'Amazing moon last night,' he said. 'Like having the lights on indoors.'

Don't doubt that kind of visitation if you are lucky enough to get one – if it is clear and strong and you can recall every detail, then someone you care about has come to spend some time with you.

After the filming was over, towards the end of September 2005, I was exhausted. That last night at the Mundays' house had really done for me. I had a couple of things to do in London and after that I went home and slept for eighteen hours, never happier than when I was in my own bed. When I got up I realized that my mind was addled and I felt confused. I was chatting to my niece in the kitchen over tea and toast, telling her what had happened at the last house, and the story became jumbled in my head. I simply couldn't remember it all clearly.

'You'd better put your feet up, Auntie Mia,' she said. 'You're showing your age.'

Cheeky monkey.

I expect the reason I was so exhausted was that I have never had so many dark, heavy spirits to deal with in such a short space of time. The production team at September had done its job and scoured the country for the worst cases it could find and sometimes during the filming it felt to me as if there was no let up. Having to be in the houses for the vigils, without opening up psychically, meant that for the first time I was experiencing these spirits as a 'normal' person would do. That had been wearing on its own, even if it was interesting for me to understand how these hauntings seem to the people who experience them. Usually, I would not have spent so long assessing each situation, but would have been able to proceed to a clearing more quickly. Also, although I have dealt with difficult, dark spirits before, I usually have a long time in between those episodes and a few easier cases on which to flex my psychic muscle. It had been a lot all at once – and a terrible demonic haunting right at the end just to really clear me out of energy.

I realized that I had also felt responsible the whole time we were filming. On the one hand it was my job to 'deliver' good TV. I had to find the ghosts and then I had to elicit their stories. On the other hand I was also responsible for everyone's safety on set, in that I was the person with the most paranormal experience, and the only psychic in the group. From the first house in Birmingham, where the atmosphere was so heavy I wasn't sure for a long time that I didn't have a demonic entity on my hands, to the final one in Salisbury where there actually was such an evil entity, I was constantly concerned that someone might fall in harm's way and that it was my job to prevent that happening.

I took Francesca's advice and plonked myself down in the most comfortable chair in the house – the one in the corner of my living room – while in my mind I ran over everything that had happened over the course of the series, glad to see that my memory was returning.

I knew that I hadn't proved what I wanted to. I knew I'd helped the families and the spirits, too. But it was on my mind that after all those hauntings, everything almost ready to air on TV, a mass of technical data that suggested quite clearly, even to the sceptical, that something was out there, I still hadn't done what I'd set out to do. The thermal images, the temperature drops, the movement sensors and the sound-recording equipment hadn't come up with anything absolutely conclusive. I had spent a lot of time with Chris on set and realized that even if I'd levitated (not that I can!), even if I'd told him details about his grandparents or given the 'perfect' reading, he wouldn't have capitulated to anything psychic being real. He would simply have put it down to good, intuitive skills and manipulation of what I already knew about him. I had teased him about it often while we were filming.

People who are sceptical will always explain things away. The world is a different place for them. The world is totally within their understanding and control. But to me it feels as if the sceptics have their eyes closed and are missing out on important things. There is a lot out there in the world to experience if you are open to it. The world is amazing.

I had big plans to spend a couple of days not even leaving the house. I was going to sleep well again that night. I knew it. I stretched out, relishing the free time I had, and then snuggled down further in the chair, really getting comfy. Then I opened up to Eric.

'Please come and talk to me,' I asked.

Eric is old. He is eighty or so. This age was Eric's prime, the time of his life that was best for him. I've never found out exactly how he lived, or when he was alive, but judging by his worn-out robes he lived a long, long time ago. The 1200s appeal to me as his era, but I don't know why. He doesn't look like a monk. More like some kind of eccentric hermit. One day I am going to go to Ireland and try to find that tower of his. When I see Eric's place and visit him in my mind, the tower is already dilapidated. The roof looks as if it is gone. I read somewhere that those towers were built near monasteries as a bolt hole in case of attack. Eric must have lived there once the threat of attack was over, because the place is a wreck and wouldn't shelter anyone! I hope the tower hasn't completely fallen apart. I hope I can recognize it.

I felt a warm sensation in the room. It is often a sensation I have around Eric when I have the time to feel it – if I call him just for a chat rather than in a crisis. I think

I get that feeling because he is someone who is completely comfortable with himself. He has a sense of age and durability – someone who is absolutely solid. When you are with Eric you feel very settled, as if what will be will be. Or rather as if what's meant to be will be. I sense that everything is very ordered around him, and everything is accepted. As I sat in the chair that feeling got stronger, increasing on his approach. Then Eric appeared in front of me.

'You can't prove things ultimately,' he said. 'It doesn't work like that.'

I lit up a cigarette and took a deep breath. I am really going to have to give up, I know. I made a mental note to buy some mints if I ever did get up out of this chair. I've tried to give up loads of times before, but I've never managed it. Nicotine patches don't work for me. I can be wearing two of them and still be puffing away. It would have to be mints and willpower. Save it for another day, I reckoned, after a week or two of no heavy ghosts, perhaps.

'Why can't I prove anything? Why not?'

'Freedom of choice. Freedom of will,' Eric said in a resigned tone. 'If people don't choose to live good lives it's their choice. If people want to live their lives only half aware of what the world truly is, then they have to be free to make that choice too.'

He was right, of course, but then that raised a question.

'But I have proof all the time. Every day. I don't have the choice not to believe. Why can't other people have the kind of proof I have?'

Eric mulled over this thorny problem for a moment.

'I don't know,' he pronounced. 'Your guess is as good as mine. But for most people, they have to be free to choose.'

I stubbed out my cigarette and wondered whether, if I yelled, one of the kids might make me another cup of tea. Sadly, Eric can't interact with the material world. That is to say, not enough to manage a kettle, milk and teabags. Besides, in the scheme of things Eric couldn't have cared less about my urge for a sip of something hot and comforting. He was totally taken up with what he was trying to explain.

'The balance of power is shifting,' he said, slightly blearily. 'People need more proof just now. There is a lot of badness in the world at this time, so there has to be more proof than before because people need it to help them draw back from evil. But not absolute proof. Not that. If you give someone absolute proof, then you rob them of their choices. You give them something today that takes away their potential tomorrow.'

He sat down on the sofa. 'And actually, Mia, you did have a choice. You could have turned away from it. Not accepted it. You didn't have to take the gift on.'

'Not much of a choice,' I mumbled, remembering how it had been.

When I started out I had asked someone practising at a spiritualist meeting to take the gift away. I had begged her, but she wouldn't. Thank goodness.

'Don't get stuck on proving things. Just help people. Help as many people as you can,' Eric finished.

I thought for a bit about the world, about what Eric said about it being out of balance, about good being out-weighed. Maybe he was right. Sometimes there is a mira-cle, of course. Sometimes, completely inexplicably, some-thing good will happen – a terminal cancer patient going into remission or someone pushing themselves beyond their limits to be able to achieve something good. We have all heard the story of a determined mother, weighing maybe a hundred and ten pounds soaking wet, who manages to lift a tonne weight to save her child's life. It is inexplicable. But it happens. Things are only absolute proof if you want to look at them that way. If I had walked out of the TV studio with pictures of a hundred angels in Trafalgar Square, someone somewhere would have said it was a trick of the light.

I settled down further into my chair and decided that being comfortable right at that moment was more important than tea. I didn't want to move. I have learned a lot from Eric. He has been a rock, really he has. I wonder sometimes what he has learned from me. 'Patience,' he said, without any hint of humour, just as I was thinking of it. And then he disappeared.

It took a good long rest to get over filming the series. I really was worn out. Just as the series started I had been doing two jobs for a couple of weeks because I had a slot on *This Morning* and was still taking private clients for readings. 'Yeah,' I thought to myself, as if only just realizing, 'No wonder I'm feeling wiped out.'

I decided that some R and R was in order and thought that after I had caught up properly with the family I would go and visit a friend in Bristol, and ease up on things for a while. At the end of the autumn I would be going on tour – forty different venues over a couple of months with 18,000 tickets to sell to fill them. I was looking forward to it, but I knew all the travelling would be crazy. For the week or so after I got home again I was still

277

dreaming about the houses in the series. I think my sub-conscious mind was simply sifting through all the infor-mation – nothing psychic about it. I dreamt about the Harrises' house and about the Elvins too.

Then, as I was getting into a better sleep pattern and had had a few days with my Mum and the girls, I got a call about another haunting. It was near Windsor. Sam had been contacted by a couple who were at their wits' end, and she passed on their details to me.

'I think you should maybe check this one out,' she said. 'It sounds pretty heavy. They really need help.' It had been more than a week without any psychic work at all and that felt like a long enough holiday to me. About time I got back to some action! I took the family's number and straight away phoned them up and had a chat. I decided that Sam was right and arranged to go and see them the next day.

Driving down to Windsor, it occurred to me how much easier it is to work without a TV crew in tow! 'This time it's just me,' I thought. There is a part of me that prefers it that way, if I'm honest. I realized in the car that dealing with people directly myself, and not having a big entourage, suddenly gave me a real sense of freedom. I arrived in Windsor and found the house – a tiny semi-detached property, just two up, two down, built around 1940. I thought it had probably been a council house to start with. 'We never would have fitted a TV crew in here anyway,' I thought to myself. It would have been nice, though, to have a runner to fix things – order pizza or alert me to the fact that my hair was in a state and I really should get the brush out.

I stood outside the front door of the house and hesitated before finally knocking. I waited for a minute and then Jenny opened it. She was a tiny brunette in her late thirties. She was beaming, though she still seemed anxious. This woman had a lot of nervous energy. Her fingers fluttered when she was standing still, as if she couldn't possibly stop moving, no matter what. She had lovely eyes. 'Thank goodness you're here,' she said.

She made us some tea and we decided to sit out in the back garden. It was still sunny then, at the end of September. Kids' toys were strewn around the paddling pool, though the kids were away. I don't like working around kids – it's not fair. I realized that for the past few weeks I had had people to arrange that kind of thing in advance – there was a researcher whose job it was to make sure any kids were away for the day and that the family were primed, knowing what to expect. I'm glad Jenny had had the good sense to send hers off for the afternoon without me having to arrange it. Not everyone understands how devastating some of these experiences can be for a young mind.

Jenny's husband, Bob, was waiting out in the back garden. He seemed more dumbfounded than anything else. He was a big bloke, around the six foot-mark, and in his mid-forties. He had an East London accent. I think he was a taxi driver. As I walked into the garden he started to talk straight off. He clearly wanted to tell me everything, but I held him off. I stopped him in his tracks because I knew enough from the scant details of our phone conversation and I wanted to see for myself. 'Why not let me have a look around first?' I suggested. 'Let me see what I can pick up.' Jenny was still fidgety. She sat down next to her husband and her hands kept flying up to her face, touching her cheek, her hair. She was chock full of energy. He just sat back solidly in his chair. 'OK,' he said. 'Whatever you want.'

I finished my tea and walked in through the back door, straight into the kitchen. There was a bathroom extension off to one side. I walked through the bathroom door and a strong feeling hit me. It was heavy and slightly sad. A name sprang into my mind – Margaret – and a vision of a woman in a long coat. I got wisps of information, as if I was walking through someone else's thoughts – ornaments moving and pictures falling. It was a strange feeling, though. I couldn't tie it to one place like I normally can. This haunting didn't seem to have a normal epicentre. When I was in the bathroom it seemed to be coming from the kitchen next door, and when I went back into the kitchen it seemed to be coming from the bathroom again. I walked around the rest of the house but there was nothing there.

Back out in the garden Jenny and Bob were eager for news.

'There's a ghost all right,' I said. 'She's called Margaret.'

Jenny sank back in her chair and stuffed her hands under her thighs. She looked pale. 'Oh God,' she said.

Bob sprang up. 'There,' he burst out. 'It's been awful. No one would believe me. Everyone thinks I'm mad. It's embarrassing.'

Bob and Jenny told me that, just as I had seen, ornaments had been moved and pictures had fallen. One day Bob turned around in the shower and he saw the woman that I had sensed, the woman in the long coat, Margaret.

'I've seen her three times – always in the bathroom – just me, no one else,' he said. 'And each time after she has appeared for a few seconds she vanishes. But there is more than that.'

Bob leaned over conspiratorially. I could tell that he hadn't had anyone sympathetic to tell this to before. There was no one nearby and yet he was acting as if we were in a crowded room. 'There's been writing on the mirror. In the steam,' he said. 'That ghost – she hates me.'

'What do you mean?' I asked.

'Everyone has seen it,' he said. 'All of us.'

'What does the writing say?'

'Well, the first word written was "Margaret". That was a while ago. But since then it's got more aggressive,' Bob says.

Jenny sat suddenly still. 'It's asking for help,' she said. 'It wants help.'

'Second time,' Bob continued, 'it was "Ouija – help me."'

'It asked you to help it by doing a ouija board?'

'Yes. After that it was "Open your veins." That ghost has taken a dislike to me, I mean I see it more than any of us. Then one Sunday it was " Get rid of Bob." Creepy. I mean, what did I ever do wrong?'

'Hold on a second,' I said. 'Just stop there.' No ghost would ask for a ouija board. This could be tricky – an entity lying about Margaret. Something like the Mundays had had.

'Jesus,' I thought, 'that would be two in two weeks.' But I wasn't sure.

I wanted to go back into the house. I left Bob and Jenny in the garden and went to stand in the doorway between the kitchen and the bathroom, right where the mirror was hanging on the back of the door – the mirror where the writing had appeared. That was the epicentre. I could feel it. That was why I had felt it coming from two rooms at once – it was in the doorway. The extension with the bathroom in it was fairly modern, and perhaps at an earlier time it had been the back door to the house. Whatever it had been in the past, the feeling there now was very strong and unpleasant. It struck me that I hadn't picked up that kind of feeling from the ghost herself. She seemed all right. What I was getting now was making me feel slightly sick. Something was wrong. I could feel it.

I stood in the doorway to the back garden. Bob and Jenny were waiting on their plastic sun chairs. 'No ghost would ask you to do a ouija board. Mostly, they don't know that they are dead, for a start,' I said. 'It doesn't tie up. Something is wrong here. I can't quite tell what yet.' My instinct, though, was that two things were going on. Margaret was a trapped spirit. Pretty standard case. But there was something else here too. And if it was asking for a ouija board it was probably demonic. I walked back into the garden.

'Actually, Mia, there's more than that,' Jenny said slowly. 'I want to show you something else.'

She disappeared past me, back into the house, and returned with stacks of photographs. The couple had been keeping their camera in the bathroom. It had been hung on a strap from the hook the mirror was secured on.

Bob said they wanted it to be handy. They took photos of the kids from time to time and photos of each other, but when the film came back from being developed there were other photographs of the empty bathroom with bright lights, blazing lights appearing out of nowhere. The lights weren't just reflections from the tiles. I leafed through the photographs and then I checked the bathroom thoroughly – there was no place for that kind of light to emanate from. The way the photos looked, the whole extension must have been glowing – the illumination was very intense, but with no obvious source. I went back out into the garden and sat down again.

'I thought the kids were doing it,' Bob said. 'Until I saw her, that is.'

'It's not your ghost. I mean, you have a ghost. Margaret is here. But I doubt she's sending you these messages. There is something else as well,' I said.

'What do you mean?'

'I don't know any more than that yet. But you have more than one thing going on here. Let's maybe deal with Margaret first, shall we? Let's go into the kitchen to do it.'

'OK. Sure.'

I decided that the best thing to do was to send her over. After all, she was definitely trapped. I stood at the worktop and centred myself.

'Don't open up too wide,' Eric said. Then I knew for sure that something else was there. But I didn't ask Eric what it was. Best to get the spirit out of the way first.

'Now I will send over Margaret to the spirit world. Don't be afraid. She is going where she belongs. She shouldn't be here. For her it will be like going home.'

Bob, Jenny and I stood in silence. I carefully opened myself up to The Zone, but I was wary. It only took a second and Margaret appeared.

'She's here,' I said.

Though they couldn't see her, both Bob and Jenny felt the temperature drop quite substantially. Jenny was rubbing her arms nervously to keep herself warm.

'Now it's time for her to leave.' I talked Bob and Jenny through what I was doing. I started to say the De Profundis.

Eric opened the portal and Margaret walked through. She didn't say anything. Not a word. However, she did seem to recognize that I could see her, and a shocked expression flickered over her face. As she went through the portal I could see that she was becoming aware of what was happening. She seemed happy. By the time I had finished the De Profundis the portal had closed. It felt right that she had gone over, and I was glad of it. A sense of elation flowed over me and I wiped away a tear. 'Bless her,' I thought, turning back into the kitchen.

'That's Margaret gone,' I told them, glad to feel the atmosphere clear momentarily. Bob and Jenny both looked delighted.

'She's gone?' Jenny said. 'Yes, it does feel different.'

And then, with a sinking feeling in my stomach, I realized that in fact, if anything, the mood felt worse. It was quite something to have two active phenomena in the house. This kind of thing is very rare anyway. But I didn't want to alarm Bob and Jenny too much. I needed time to think.

'I feel a change too,' I said. 'But it hasn't only been Margaret here. There is something else as well. I need to deal with that next. I think that job might take me a while.'

I asked Bob and Jenny to go back into the garden and I sat in the kitchen smoking a cigarette as I talked to Eric and tried to figure it out. Whatever was now in the kitchen, or indeed, nearby, didn't feel exactly Evil. It was almost more like the threat of Evil. And I couldn't feel a spirit. There was nothing human here. I walked back through the bathroom doorway and my stomach lurched with dread. Then I walked back again. Same. The spot around the doorway felt menacing, but only two feet away everything felt fine. I knew something was causing that feeling, only nothing was there. It was very confusing.

'Well?' I asked Eric. 'You're going to have to fill me in. I can't guess.'

Eric looked as if he was thinking for a moment or two.

'There isn't anything there,' he said. 'Not exactly. It's not a portal. Some places, though, are closer to the other side. It's as if the lining is thinner. Perhaps something particularly bad happened here and some kind of connection was made. It's not a door to somewhere else. But it could be. There is something in there that wants to break through. It's trying to get in and it has found somewhere there is a weakness. It's the mirror.'

'Is what wants to break through something evil?' I asked. Evil is quite another thing. But this evil wasn't here, wasn't out. It was contained – trying to break through but not there yet.

Eric nodded.

I was glad that I didn't have to contain it. Having to deal with an entity right then would have been like doing another episode of *Haunted Homes* and honestly, I was not fully enough recovered from so many heavy experiences in the space of eight weeks to take it on. I had no desire to add another one to my tally if I didn't have to.

'Brilliant,' I said to Eric as I realized this was something Bob and Jenny could deal with on their own. They simply needed to close off the portal by getting rid of their mirror.

I went back into the garden and I explained to the couple as best I could.

'The ghost won't come back, though?' Jenny wanted confirmation. She didn't seem to understand that the ghost was the least of their worries.

'No,' I said. 'But you have this other entity that wants to break through and that would be far worse than having a ghost. It can't come on its own so it wants an invitation and that's why it asked you to do the ouija board. I can't tell you how terrifying that would be. You need to remove the camera from the bathroom and the mirror too. For some reason, those things have been attracting it. I don't know why. Keep everything away from the door and I am sure it will settle down.'

While I was there Bob put the mirror in the garden shed and Jenny took the camera upstairs. When I left they were fine.

A couple of weeks later I was at home again, preparing myself for the tour, and I received a frantic phone call from Bob and Jenny. They sounded terrified, passing the phone between each other. Bob had put the mirror back in the bathroom – 'We need a mirror in there,' he said, as if that was a logical explanation. As soon as the mirror went back up the writing started again, even more abusive than ever. 'It said, "Bob must die",' he told me. Then, that morning, Bob saw a thin trickle of blood come from the centre of the mirror and slip down the glass.

'What did I tell you?' I shouted. 'You can't have a mirror on that door.'

As far as I could figure out, the mirror was acting as some kind of magnet. All ghosts, all entities for that matter, are energy. Now, I need to be completely clear here, I have never had a case like this one before. In my view, mirrors are not inherently dangerous. But that mirror, in that place, was acting as a conduit for something evil. It was a focus for it. I was certain that, more than anything, the mirror should not be there.

Standing in the kitchen, talking on the phone, I had a strong sense of worry. In fact I was worrying myself sick about Bob and Jenny even as I spoke to them. I was worried for their kids too. But I was also furious. It seemed so stupid. 'If you have to get a mirror, just get a plastic one and don't hang it anywhere near the door,' I said. But that didn't seem to be Bob's problem. Not really.

'None of our friends believe us,' Bob said, as if this was an explanation.

It seemed as if this was the worst thing for him, and it was clear to me that he didn't realize the danger he was in. This wasn't a human spirit, it was an evil entity. It had only dark, evil desires – to escape into the world and to wreak any kind of cruelty and havoc that it could.

Bob shouldn't have been issuing an invitation like this, he should not have been providing a conduit – it was so dangerous.

I decided to go back to Windsor that evening, and this time I took my friend, Alan. When we got there I came on very heavy but I wanted to really make the point. It was so unsafe for them and I was very concerned.

It is difficult to handle an evil entity. For me, all three times I have had to do it, it has proved a big challenge. Each time afterwards I have felt completely wiped out. I didn't want to handle any more if I could help it. With spirits, if ever I were to fail to send one over, there might be a tantrum, if you like. A bit of paranormal activity, perhaps. With an entity, if I didn't get it right, I couldn't say what harm might come from it.

Back in Windsor with Alan, I sat in the kitchen with Bob and Jenny and explained that their family stood to come to some real harm. Calling something up by mistake was one thing, but deciding to do so deliberately was quite another. I had the sense of this being like a lion in a cage. They were taunting it and if it got out it would cause serious damage. These entities are violent – physically violent – if they are allowed their way.

Alan and I gave them a really strong talking to and in the end Bob put the mirror out of the house and into the garden, and removed the camera (which had also gone back into the bathroom as part of Bob's drive to obtain proof to show his friends he wasn't mad). Alan and I stayed for a while longer because I really wanted to hammer the point home. This thing was dangerous. They had to stay away. They really mustn't encourage it.

'You mustn't do anything to attract it and then it will go away,' I said. 'It wants to get out, but it can't unless you invite it. You are safe, just don't put that mirror back,' I warned. 'It's using it somehow. Don't give it the opportunity.'

I couldn't imagine they would be that stupid again. The next day the trouble had settled down.

Another week passed and then out of the blue there was another phone call. The couple had put the mirror back. Again. And of course the trouble had started all over.

'It is evil. You do understand that,' I pressed them.

'I missed it,' said Bob. 'I wanted to prove to my mates that it really exists. I wanted to get a photo.'

By this stage I was fuming. The way he was trying to explain what he had done suggested that he really believed that I was going to tell him he was completely right, and putting the mirror back was entirely under-standable. This time the lights had been going on and off around the house. Bob had been pushed on the stairs. It was so violent that he had nearly fallen. Jenny had been feeling sick. The kids couldn't sleep.

'No bloody wonder,' I shouted down the phone.

I was terrified that they were going to let this thing loose, and then I would have to go in there and face it down. It seemed so unnecessary.

'It will settle down,' I said, 'if you just keep the mirror out of the bathroom and the kitchen. Don't talk about it, don't give the entity any energy. It can't get out unless you invite it, but if you keep on like you're doing you might inadvertently manage that.'

'I want to prove it's there. No one believes me,' Bob whined.

'There's no point in me coming over there,' I snapped. 'And I think you are being very, very foolish. You have children in that house and you are putting them and yourselves through this for nothing but vanity. If you won't stop it for your own sakes then stop it for your kids. For heaven's sake,' I begged them, 'just take the mirror down and keep the camera away.'

In the end they promised once again. I don't make a habit of phoning people and checking up once I have been somewhere. This time, though, I reckoned a call would be in order now and again. And in the meantime if they needed me, I had no doubt that they would be in touch.

My cardinal rule these days is Don't Dabble. The spirit world is a wonderful reality. That you can be visited out of love by people who have passed over to it is, to me, inspiring. A beautiful mystery. The other place, though: now that isn't something to mess around with. Don't dabble, whatever you do.

In the meantime, my mind set to wandering. I wondered what had happened in that doorway that made it a weak link. What had happened that made it possible for some awful entity to try to break through? It must have been something dreadful, I reckoned. I found myself speculating on what it must be like on the other side of that closed window, being desperate to get to the other side, clawing to get out, compelled by Evil to kill and destroy. I had never seen a place like that before, nor have I seen one since.

'It's rare, isn't it?' I asked Eric.

'Yes,' he said. 'Mostly the world is cut off from other places, spiritual realms. You don't see it. You're not supposed to.'

Having had that experience of Bob and Jenny – watching someone with the absolute urge to prove something, no matter how dangerous it might be to themselves or to others really made me think about my own urge to prove things. In fact, it has made me a lot more laid back about it. After all, before I got my gift I would never have believed there was a spirit world. I had never believed in Good and Evil. As far as I was concerned that was old-fashioned mumbo jumbo: the kind of thing that we learned about at Sunday school as kids. If I didn't believe it before, then why should I push it on anyone else? People have a fantastic ability to take on as much as they can at any time. People will come to it when they're ready – if they're ready. That is the main thing.

On a hook above my bed I have a dream catcher and a bundle of religious symbols. I have a Star of David and a Celtic Cross. I have a Muslim crescent and an image of the Buddha. I like to think I am sleeping with a spiritual beacon above my head that says, 'Here is someone dedicated to Good.' I find myself completely non-denominational. At the core of all religious faiths is a belief in God and a belief in good, which in the end is the same thing. To me that's all that matters.

When people come to me for a reading I just try to see the good in them and not judge what they have done. Eric says that life is about yesterday, today and tomorrow. So many people live only for today – that's just the way they are. Especially emotionally speaking. They don't give too much consideration to where they have come from and what they have done or, for that matter, the consequences that lead on to tomorrow. I think that's a crucial step for people. I think that for many people that is a first step – the realization that it isn't all Me Me Me and Now Now Now.

Someone might have lived a bad life up until today, and because of something they have realized they might be on their way to a good life tomorrow. There is always hope. I truly believe that. I once got into correspondence with a man in prison who had done terrible things. He was a murderer and a torturer. His life had been very black. He regretted what he had done but he hadn't come to terms with it. He told me he was thinking of killing himself. That was the only thing he could think to do. *Wouldn't it be better*, he wrote, *if I wasn't here?* He was serving a sentence that meant he would never get out of jail, and as far as he was concerned that meant he would never be able to make up for what he had done. We corresponded over a long period of time. I told him you can always do something. Killing yourself is just a cop out. You don't get to choose when you are born and you shouldn't get to choose when you die. If you truly regret and are truly sorry, then you can always make up for what you have done. Even if it is only in a small way. Day to day in that prison, maybe he could help people. At least he still had a chance to make amends, even if the good things he had the opportunity to do now weren't on the scale of the bad things he had done previously. *Just don't bottle out*, I wrote. *Take it on*.

In the end, of course, everyone is going to die. Every one of us will look back on our lives and our relationships. It's a shame that so many people only consider what they have done when it's too late. Imagine the possibilities for change that exist in being aware of what you are doing now. Of making changes now. It's difficult, I know. But I think you can make the decision to help people no matter where you are or what situation you are in. Like that convict, you might sink so low that on a scale of one to ten you are only a one or a two, but then you can fight your way back, help people, make different choices, and you might end up being a four or a five. And that's an improvement worth making.

I wonder what the experience of being haunted will have done for each of the families in the series. I'd never wish a haunting on anyone, but still it must change those families somehow. Perhaps it made them realise what they had or simply gave them an awareness of the spirit world that will give them strength if they need it. I wish them well.

Every day I realize that people are amazing. The human spirit is amazing. I walk down the street and I see beautiful auras in all colours. I saw a purple, silver and gold aura on a thirteen-year-old girl the other day. She must have been an old soul, an experienced spirit. She probably didn't know all the strength and beauty she was carrying within her. The sixth sense is the last magic on earth and it's inside all of us.

The Gift

*The story of an ordinary woman's
extraordinary power*

Mia Dolan

Mia Dolan was 22 when she first heard the voice of her spirit guide. Brought up in an ordinary working-class community on the Isle of Sheppey, she had always been down-to-earth and certainly never believed in psychic phenomena. Now that the voice had spoken to Mia, strange things began to happen: she 'left' her body and walked through the house, she 'saw' a plane crash in horrific detail, only to hear it reported on the news that evening. She thought she was going insane.

Finally, Mia accepted that she had a rare psychic gift and learned how to control and use it. A few years later, Mia's courage was tested when she tragically foresaw the murder of her own brother and had to endure the loss of her young son.

The gift is the compelling story of an ordinary woman's extraordinary gift – an inspirational life lived with raw honesty, humour and compassion.

ISBN 0 00 715451 8

Available now in all good bookstores

Mia's World

An extraordinary gift. An unforgettable journey.

Mia Dolan with Rosalyn Chissick

'Will you teach me to be psychic?'

Would I teach her? 'It would take time,' I told her. 'And you would have to keep an open mind. One of the major keys to unlocking the sixth sense is belief. Belief is a magic word.'

'How long would it take?'

'Six months,' I decided. 'Six months from sceptic to psychic.'

When Mia Dolan, one of Britain's most gifted psychics, agreed to meet Rosalyn, a writer and journalist, she wasn't intending to take on a student of clairvoyance. Her student wasn't expecting to be thrust headlong into a world of mind-reading, ghost-hunting and foretelling the future – or to see the mysteries of the afterlife revealed. From that day the two women embarked on a breathtaking adventure that changed them both for ever...

ISBN 0 00 720892 8

Available now in all good bookstores